Scott & Martha

Outta My Mind

Enjoy—

All the best—

[illegible]

2013

Outta My Mind

J. W. Gustafson

ESSAYS ON LIFE ◆ VOLUME ONE

Outta My Mind

ISBN: 978-0-9849175-0-1

Proclaim Publications
25 Liberty Street
Haverhill, Massachusetts 01832

Book & Cover Design: Kim Gardell
Cover Image: "The Thinker" by Auguste Rodin (1840-1917)

Preface

Do thoughts roam around in your head as they do in mine? In the middle of the night they poke you into wakefulness? Or on a plane or in a taxi your train of thought hurtles around corners on two wheels? At the awkwardest times flashes of insight, though not always brilliant, streak like shooting stars through the brain. How many times have I groped for a pen in the dark lest I lose a thought?

These things happen to me all the time. I think of this book as a sort of download to free up space on my cranial hard drive for fresher musings.

I hope you find them worth reading. What follows is more a hodge-podge of discreet topics rather than a unified story.

I've enjoyed writing them. I hope you may find something of significance for yourself here.

I am hoping what follows is an exception to the old adage, Better to be silent and thought a fool rather than to speak and remove all doubt.

Some of these essays are whimsical; others are stream-of-consciousness that relate a moment of elevation in my journey along life's path. A few are serious attempts at philosophical or theological profundity.

You can browse here. No need to go from start to finish.

Should you have comments I would enjoy hearing from you, *jgustafson@necc.mass.edu*

Outta My Mind

Table of Contents

The King's Open House

There once was a good-hearted king who thought it his duty to see to the well-being of his people.

He cared so deeply for their welfare that he proclaimed an open invitation for any of his subjects to come to the palace at any time day or night to meet with him.

His neighbors asked John Goodman if he was planning any time soon to visit the king. "Oh Yes!" he replied, "but I must get myself together and be ready."

At times when he felt troubled, John would get out his best suit of clothes and start brushing so he would be proper for his visit with the king.

But then some diversion would come. He would distract himself with pleasures at hand with his buddies.

Soon his troubles got deeper and John decided he would indeed go to the king.

But he noticed his clothes needed some mending in places. And the waist needed to be let out on his good suit so he would look trim and not be bulging at the seams in the king's presence.

So time went by.

Finally John was so distressed by his circumstances that he put the best touches he could on his suit, polished his well-worn shoes to hide the scuffs, and set out for the palace.

"I still am ashamed to look like this before the king. But I am so in need of his help that I will take the risk now."

As he approached the palace he was met at the gate by a guard. "Why have you come?" asked the guard.

"I have summoned my courage and cleaned up as best I can in these old garments and have come for the open invitation of our king. I hope I am not so un-presentable as to be turned away."

"That's no matter," said the guard. "Do you see that huge pile of old clothing by the palace walls? That is the clothing of all who have come before you. The king does not look upon the sorry garments of his people. He has each one strip down and be dressed in garments of silk and gold that the king provides them."

"Oh, I wish I had known that!" said John.

"No matter," replied the guard. "You are too late now anyway. The king has taken all the subjects who have come and sailed off to a new world to establish a better kingdom. The gates here are closed by the Usurper who has taken control and intends to ravage the land."

"How dreadful!" John remonstrated. "What is to become of me now? Why didn't the king send officers to arrest me and take me by force if he knew the day was approaching? Now I am left here at the mercy of this Usurper you mention with nothing but these rags to cover me."

"I know little of that," said the guard. "But I know the king would never force people to come to his presence. I wish you well, sir, but there is nothing I can do for you."

Give and It Will Be Given Unto You

Each year in Kenya, I room with another happy bachelor (temporarily so and not by desire), Reverend George Mitchell, PhD. Many a Baptist Union church he has served in Scotland over the decades knows this is a man of God whom to know is to love.

One token of his esteem is that he does over 60 funerals a year. You see, George grew up with the toughs of Glasgow and he loves the common man. They turn to him, especially if they have not been the church-going type. They know he understands the edgier side of life and can speak fearlessly yet with compassion to those who have lost their way and need a Pilot of the Soul. And we all know Who that is.

We love him here at Scott Theological College. He is a silver-tongued smithy of words, often enhancing his message with power point slides. He writes booklets that he sells to a small market of those he comes in contact with wherever he goes.

But the most endearing thing about George—did I mention also that he plays a respectable trumpet and has a fine singing voice?—is that he does works of compassion all the time. It's in his blood.

As he goes about Scotland, where he is a popular speaker, he advocates for the poor in Kenya. And people give him money and clothing to stuff into his wallet and bags for the needy when he comes each January.

Not that he's perfect. Without his wife, Jean, he'd be at sixes and sevens most of the time. I know. I live with guy for three weeks every other year.

But he has a wonderful sense of humor and can tell stories without taking a breath for hours on end. It's a fine tonic just to pal around with him.

Here's what he did the last few days of this week.

He went off with Vundi to talk to the leaders of a local Anglican diocese about the biblical work ethic. You see people here just pray for rain when they could be developing local irrigation that could save crops and lessen starvation. At the end of his seminar he hands over 250,000 Kenya shillings for an agricultural project Dr. Vundi is spearheading to help the rural folk grow more food. George has touted this when people back home want to reward George for his ministry to them. "I'll take it to Africa."

George goes down to visit the gate men—morning and often evening. He has a bag. "Take some socks - or maybe a shirt. Here's a bit o'dosh for you." "Oh thank you—I'll be buying food with it today for my family."

He goes out to the town football pitch (soccer field) to meet the coach and cheer the local kids. "Could you use some uniforms?"

So he goes with the coach downtown and buys shirts, shorts, socks in bright colors like that of the Brazil team. "Now—could you cut and collect some of the grass here to improve your field and feed some cows the college keeps?" "Oh sure, Dr. Mitchell, we'll do just that." Their eyes are big. They never dreamed they could have uniforms! "You look like Brazil now," says George, "go play like them then!"

George has bags of ties and scarves to sprinkle about among the students and faculty and staff here. And some shirts and pencils, and dresses and even a suit or two. Whatever he can gather from folk or buy in the thrift.

Each afternoon a tap on the door signals the kids have come looking for a balloon from George's pocket. "What do you say?" he asks with a broad grin. "Thank you!" they whisper.

Here is a man who teaches Hebrew and Greek, New Testament, and numerous other courses in a college in Glasgow. Now retired, he has known from his youth what it is to be in want and he is doing all he can for others in need. He's not wealthy himself. But people trust him to deliver the goods to the poorest of the poor as well as to needs of all kinds. Some people talk about the plight of the poor. George does something about it.

There's a story about a guy in Wisconsin who was a fabulous fisherman. When others were skunked he always came home with something—every time. A suspicious game warden asked how he did it. "Come on out with me and I'll show you."

So on a day they put out into the middle of the little lake and let down the anchor. The man pulls out a stick of dynamite, lights it, and hands it toward his companion. "You can't do that!"

The warden screams. "Fishing by stunning them is against the law!!!" "Look," says the other, still holding out the sizzling TNT, "are you going talk or fish?"

George is a guy who is always fishing. He is a wonderful talker you can listen to all day. But he walks the walk. For Jesus. For the least of these.... For those who are invisible as they stand to the side in the shadows while we fly on by on our important errands.

"You will be fishers of men," Someone once promised.

Am I talking? Or am I fishing? He's holding out the sizzling stick of Gospel dynamite to me—yes to me.

A Marriage Made in Heaven

The couple that has a house church in Dehradun had me for dinner last night. We ate a bit early for them—8 PM. I told Sooraj that at home I would be thinking of stoking the fire and going up to bed about now.

His wife, Preeti, fixed a great meal. And this for me—a guy who struggles with most Indian food—not enough raw veggies and always the pepper and curry is a bit too hot in most dishes. But this was really good! The only thing that burned my virgin lips was some chicken bought at a market. Sooraj had asked that they hold back on the spice. They said OK. But it still left my lips tingling—a sensation not often felt since my younger days—but then let's not go there.

So I felt really at home with these friends of several years now. I was teasing everyone. Sooraj said, "I like your sense of humor." I don't hear that much anymore.

We got talking about our families. I mentioned how I have three granddaughters in their mid-twenties and none yet married. Maybe I should put a marriage ad in the newspapers here and see if I can find someone. They need some help. The papers here have 4 pages with about 200 ads hawking the age, looks, caste, education and religion of women—and a few men, too. I guess the matchmakers in the USA are not keeping up with their responsibilities.

"Really? You have that in USA?" Sooraj asks. No – but we do have online match making. Even one of my friends found a Christian soul mate wife that way—and they are very happy. "Do you know any nice Indian guys who are Christians who might take a wife from the USA?"

He laughed.

But since we were on the subject, Preeti came in (wives serve during the meal, so she was not at table with us and the two kids), sat down and started bubbling over with her story.

She is a native of Dehradun, while Sooraj hails from 200 miles south. She was getting into her mid-twenties. That's when families do a full-court press to get their girls to the goal line.

One prospect was a guy from a well-connected family. His mother was a politician and her father successful in his career. So they had means. Negotiations got under way.

Preeti's parents said there was one obstacle—they had no money for the usual dowry. This is a constant concern in India. The girl should bring assets to the guy's family. But they were told that would not be necessary. Preeti would make a fine wife for their son. They need not anti-up with a dowry. Your daughter has a degree as well as advanced computer skills. She is a fine match for him. So the engagement was announced. A wedding date set. And the couple was to start getting to know each other.

Now one must realize that an engagement here is much like in Bible times. Do you recall how Joseph, betrothed to Mary, actually had to take a public action when he wanted out due to her pregnancy? He resolved to do it privately—showing the kind heart he had toward her.

But in Preeti's case there proved to be no kind hearts. The parents suddenly started making demands. Preeti's folks would pay for the wedding and the huge feast that goes with it. They were to provide all the furnishings for the newlyweds' house. When there was some hesitation over this change in expectations the mother of the guy would phone repeatedly and yell and scream why they were not willing to do as custom requires? Preeti's parents were crushed—but had no way out since the engagement had been published abroad.

As Preeti, meanwhile, was getting to know her intended better, she began to have reservations—not just for her parents' position but for herself. Her intuition sent up warnings. She found he was an alcoholic, for one thing. The future father-in-law is from Punjab—an area notorious for "accidental" burnings of young wives over dowry displeasure. She began to become depressed. Telling her parents her feelings she asked for them to break off the arrangement.

They did so. And all hell broke loose. Her relatives were shamed—how could you do this to our family name? And the guy's parents loosed a torrent of false accusations about Preeti to the gossip mills. Preeti now crawled into a dark hole of despair. She thought, maybe I should just end my life.

At the time, Preeti was a Roman Catholic, so she knew where the answer lay although she was not truly converted. She began to call to Jesus for help. She had a Bible in the house that her father used to read from to the family. Only God can take her through this darkness. She starts to attend a Brethren church nearby, with a pastor who preaches the Gospel. She is somewhat confused still and has the cloud of suicide swirling in her mind.

The pastor's wife senses her distress and invites her to come to their home. The floodgates open in this safe place. She weeps for nearly an hour while the pastor's wife just holds her and prays for her. Consolation and counsel follow. She gives it all to Jesus—whatever he has for her, even if she never marries.

In time she goes to work at the complex where the lepers have a cottage industry to support themselves, established by the Catholic Church years ago. There is a young man who comes regularly to do outreach ministry to the people there—who have little outside contact and no hope for integration into society. He is soon to start a church next door that the lepers can walk to. This is Sooraj, studying for ministry at New Theological College. They of course talk over lunch breaks and so on.

Some of their mutual friends see a match here. So one arranges for them to come to her home and meet in a proper way. Preeti is skittish, but agrees to come. Her parents even say it is OK for him to take her for coffee and talk there.

But Sooraj is extremely shy talking with a girl. "No—we'll meet here," he says.

So they share each other's testimony. Preeti is careful to confess the sorry business about her disgraced engagement fiasco. Sooraj, undaunted, expresses interest in her.

But Preeti has been burned—badly—by her ordeal. She is not sure. The trauma is still with her. She prays, asking for guidance. Sooraj is a believer. She will accept him if God indicates. God seems to be saying, "Yes." Uncle George and Auntie Leela of New Theological College encourage the couple. "They will be right for each other."

So the decision is made and a date set for nuptials.

Now preparation must go forward. Preeti's parents will have to get everything ready. Lots of shopping for their daughter, lots of planning.

But Preeti cannot find it in herself to take part. No shopping for her. She starts going to her room and reading the Psalms. She lights a candle to remind her of her need for light from above. For ten days she sequesters herself. She reads all 150 Psalms ten times during that fortnight. The candle burns out every time.

Wedding bells start ringing. She is putting on her veil. Still unsure, she keeps saying, "Lord, I am in your hands." And then it happens.

As she and Sooraj start exchanging vows and rings, the joy of the Lord sweeps into her heart. A peace pushes all the darkness away. She is ecstatic. *This is right!* Beaming now with animation, she is coming home to the safe place in her Heavenly Father's provision and in Sooraj's love.

As Preeti finishes her story she is radiant before us. She is a beautiful woman, with a boy of 5 and a girl of 3. And they love the Lord so deeply and serve the poor and lowly with such devotion. He was 27 when they married, she 26. While they work on the campus now, they still minister to the people in and around the lepers' home downtown, where I have preached several times over the last few years.

Sooraj asks me to pray for them before I leave.

As I walk the hundred paces back to the guesthouse, my heart is elated. God brings his people through their dark hours. She needed this trauma to get serious with Jesus. Once again, God brings good from the bad. The heavenly Father arranged this union when earthly parents could not find a way. What a beautiful couple.

The meal was scrumptious, to be sure. But we feasted mostly on a heavenly food that nourishes not bodies but souls.

Ideas Have Consequences

Philosophy—what about it? It can make you pull your hair out. Or tie your mind in knots. Or shed light on your path.

Some say philosophy is over. These are the post-modernists of our time. There is no truth, they say. We all just grab some ideas that we like, or that comfort us, until in the end we croak, and that's about it. No truth can be found. Some say philosophy can give insights into what is really going on in the world and help us to shape a flourishing life.

Key Question One: What is the basis for *any conclusions* we adopt? For many the basis is no more than this. "What makes me feel good today?" Truth doesn't matter. To each his own. The only "sin" is being critical of someone else's ideas.

For philosophers like me the basis for any conclusions I am going to embrace is what stands up to tough questioning. Are my ideas about things logically defensible (coherent)? Are they inclusive (comprehensive)? Are they workable (pragmatic)?

Key Question Two: Is there a reality beyond my own imagining that I should pay attention to? Or is the universe whatever I would like it to be?

Examples. "I truly believe I'm not high and can drive home." Result: I am sincere, but dead—another road kill.

"I truly believe I can cheat on my spouse and not hurt anyone." Result: devastation for my kids and myself.

"I sincerely believe that when I die there is nothing more to it."

Result: Hmmmm....

"I truly think that if I am a good person, I'll be OK if there is a final exam after death." Result: Hmmmm....

My viewpoint: I had better examine everything with rigor, because the world/the universe/reality is what it is, and my thinking either helps me to get in line with forces bigger than myself or I could be crushed. I could be sincere but fatally wrong. That would not be good.

Key Question Three: What is the nature of what is? I am in a universe that blows my mind when I think about it—everything from quarks to galaxies. How best explain all this?

Key Question Four: I am going to die, that's for sure. What is the wisest plan I can come up with for my life?

I suppose I could ignore it all. "Who knows the answer?" But maybe that's too big a risk.

I, for one, want to think about the meaning of my life as a whole; about the value of my life when all is said and done and the lid of the coffin closes over me. About the purpose that I choose for myself: why am I here and why am I doing what I am doing? At my age I could be playing golf in Arizona or fishing in Florida every day.

Let's call these big questions the quest for **Meaning/Value/Purpose.**[1]

Some say there is no **Meaning/Value/Purpose** that is based in what's out there. The universe has no **Meaning/Value/Purpose.**

---

1 MVP Most Valued Parameters?

That means there is no **Meaning/Value/Purpose** to be *discovered*—you have to *make up your own* **Meaning/Value/Purpose.**

If this is the truth, then philosophy comes to a stop sign—*Dead End.* Do what you want and hope you luck out by not being born in Bangladesh or Baghdad and not getting Dengue Fever or lung cancer or being taken out by a drunk or a terrorist.

Of old this philosophy of life was *Eat, drink, and be merry, for tomorrow we die.* Why not? "Works for me" you may be saying. But are you *sure* it will work out for you?

Others say the ultimate reality out there is packed with **Meaning/Value/Purpose**. We are not just going—we are all going *somewhere.* The meaning of life is to do whatever it takes to get in line with a Grand Reality that promises a hope and future. Values we choose either support this quest or de-rail it. There is a purpose for my existence, for our existence. So what we embrace has *eternal implications.* It's like deciding which way to run when a volcano explodes. One direction may lead to safety, the other to a river of hot magma.

This is the big debate in philosophy. And not every answer can be correct.

Either the universe is much ado about nothing (in the end when the galaxies run out of gas and the law of entropy brings about a steady state just above absolute zero) or it is pregnant with endless life and value for us.

What clues, what evidence can we find in what little we have to work with here on planet Earth? Science cannot resolve this, because science rests on philosophical assumptions that may or may not be true. Sorry—but that's the way it is.

So what is the bottom line?

We need to think long and carefully despite our busy, even frenetic lives. That is what philosophy is all about. It is about the quest for truth—the quest for **Meaning/Value/Purpose.**

Going Home

It is time for me to go home from India. One of my students, Suraj Lepcha, offers to ride along as Anil drives me to the Dehradun airport over an hour away. I am glad for the offer, since Anil knows about 25 words of English and I know 3 words in Hindi.

Lepcha by contrast speaks good English. He is one of the students who sat in the front row for 36 hours of lecture with his eyes bugging out and writing down every word I said. He tells me how my style captured him, while the content filled his heart as well as mind. I have seen the philosophy bug bite a student here and there in my adjunct teaching experience. Lepcha is one.

So I ask him to tell me his story. By now we are choking on the smoggiest air since I arrived on October 22. Anil is dodging dogs, cows, bikes, trucks, and pedestrians in downtown Dehradun—as usual.

Lepcha tells me he is from Nepal. Obviously he is oriental—but then several eastern states in India nestle against Myanmar, not far from Vietnam. So he could as easily be Indian.

How did he get to this college? Well, it is actually not that far in miles, since Nepal borders India and Tibet. He has a sponsor—a woman in Germany. He calls her Mum.

My curiosity goes up a notch. Tell me more.

"Actually, I am technically an orphan. My father was an alcoholic and took his own life when I was three years of age. My mother then abandoned me. A teacher in a Catholic school gave me shelter and helped me go to school. But my mind was messed up. I started doing drugs and ruining my life as a young teen.

"There are churches near where I live. Christians from Germany came to hold some meetings for youth. That's how I became a Christian. But it was still very hard. Everyone always wants to know your family—who are your parents? What could I say? If I say I am with the teacher, they would say bad things, for they know he is not married. And obviously, my parents are not from Germany.

"So I was lonely—almost an outcast. Then the Lord called me to serve him, and I came to this college. Mum pays my fees, but it is hard with no one near to belong to. I told Mum I want to study and get to the top.

She is so wise. She said that is OK, but pray for the Lord to show you what he wants for you. So I realized I was being driven to get recognized, and with that get acceptance and love. But now God is showing me a way. I want to go back to Nepal to the poor area

I come from and start a school, since kids out there have little chance to get an education."

That's so great, I say. Because there is a way to get churches started here in north India. Will that work in Nepal?

"Oh yes. Buddhists and Hindus—and Muslims, too—want their kids to get ahead so they will not always live hand to mouth."

Lepcha is musical—playing by ear. He plays bass guitar in the New Theological College praise team. Lots of talent. He knows that music is a way to build a base. Most of the Christians in Nepal are young people—not too many of their parents have come to faith.

Lepcha has a keen mind. He says the course opened up something he had been yearning for, even though he didn't know what his mind was craving. He is persistent, too. He asked good questions of me. And if I did not hit the target he kept on asking. In fact, he tells me he is like that, and some of his friends get tired of his persistence in their dorm sessions. He keeps pressing until his mind is satisfied.

By now we are well out in the country and the air is easier to breathe. I see a small control tower ahead on the left. The hour has flown by—except for Anil, who has to watch everything like a hawk. He has to pass slow traffic on this narrow, busy road—always a "white knuckler" for me. So I am glad to be distracted by conversation.

I am eager to have Lepcha stay in touch. I can perhaps encourage his potential. I think he will make an impact in Nepal in areas not yet touched by the Gospel.

I give him my card with the e-mail contact. "I will have an e-mail waiting for you when get to the USA tomorrow!"

We park at the terminal—if you can call it that. Just a low building with a scanner for bags and one check-in desk. Kingfisher Air has only two flights a day.

Just before I go past the officer guarding the entrance, I have Anil take a photo of me and Lepcha, my only Nepalese student so far.

Well, it's time to go. I will trust myself to the worldwide airlines system, expecting it to deliver me to Logan in Boston in about 24 transit hours.

This is what is significant: A week before I left for India in October, I struggled with the feeling that I really did not want to go. But I was committed, so there was no question of not making the journey.

Looking back, I realize that something did not want me to come here—trying to derail this mission that seems, to my surprise, to have touched more students in a significant way than was true of my previous six stints at New Theological College.

But God helped me not to listen to that temptation.

So now I keep giving God a "smile offering." I cannot get over the things he is doing here that he has shown to me.

With a joyous heart, I'm going home.

Give Thanks in All Circumstances

This admonition from the Apostle sounds well and good. But is it realistic, one is tempted to ask? Terrible things can happen for which one cannot be thankful.

True, but the command says to give thanks to God, not to be thankful for the situation *per se*. And we have to admit—St. Paul actually did this despite the incredible hardships he endured. It is not cheap advice he is giving us.

Professor Solomon Bison invited me to tea today, where his wife, Ruby, told me of her bout with cancer. She was eager to tell me, since she knows I am a cancer survivor myself, having had prostate surgery in 1999.

She was diagnosed on June 17, the day before her birthday and scheduled for treatment the next day. Her friends unexpectedly came that same day with her gifts and they were able to celebrate before she had to leave on the train next morning.

But she was apprehensive, naturally, as I had been, praying, "Lord will I be OK or is this my time?" But in a dream that night God indicated he would be with her and she would survive. Something similar had comforted me ten years ago.

Tests soon showed that she had ovarian cancer. They would operate and take her ovary, several surrounding lymph nodes, and part of her stomach lining.

However as she went for the testing, she and Solomon were worrying about the expenses. If she had to stay in Delhi for tests and then surgery and recovery they would never be able to meet the costs. They decided to trust God for that and go forward.

She met a Christian nurse who told her about an experienced surgeon who was local and who made a fast track for her to see him ahead of four others waiting for a consultation. He assured her that her condition was treatable and he could do it locally at half the cost—about 100,000 rupees.

Friends at the college here, even students, hearing of her need had contributed 50,000 rupees. They needed double that. They were encouraged that God would supply the finances.

A pastor came to pray with them and left an envelope with Solomon with the warning not to lose it or let the children find it since it had some money in it. After leaving the pastor phoned and asked, "Did you guard the envelope?" "Oh yes, but I have not had time to count yet." The next day he got an e-mail asking the same question. Expecting a small gift from the pastor, he opened the seal and counted. To his astonishment it came to 55,000 rupees, meeting their immediate need with 5,000 extra! God was taking care as promised.

She was set for an MRI. But as she was being prepped she coughed. The doctors asked about that. When she told them her condition, they canceled the MRI since if she should have a coughing fit during the procedure it would have to be done again later, doubling the expense. Once again, the expenses were cut down for her.

The doctors operated to remove the ovary, some lymph nodes and adjacent parts of her stomach. Lab tests would later show cancer only in the ovary—very good news.

But as she was being brought out of anesthesia suddenly her pulse went to zero and her breathing stopped. The doctors rushed in to get her to a room with oxygen and so forth. Solomon was panicking. The doctors ordered him to leave the surgical theatre.

During this time she was in a lot of pain, since she could not tolerate the usual painkillers. She was so exhausted from the long ordeal. Then a most unusual experience came to her.

When her heart stopped beating she saw a table with a line down the middle. Her body lay on one side of this line while she was on the other. A voice called to her. "If you are tired, just come to me." She knew it was Jesus speaking to her. "Oh, that would be so nice to rest and go into your presence in heaven."

"Just come, then."

She could see a long line of funeral cars leaving the West Gate of the college.

"But the people at the college will be so sad! And my husband and young children—who will care for them? God, I need to go back...!" She was shouting now.

Someone placed a hand on her shoulder.

"Ruby! You are back—you are going to be OK." The doctor was gently shaking her shoulder as she opened her eyes.

The doctor said she was "dead" for several minutes—no pulse, no breathing. And then she got a weak pulse that gradually got stronger. In a short time she was out of danger.

The next day in the ward recovering, she could not sleep. Nurses urged her to get some rest. But there was a child in the ward who would not eat. His father was in tears, expecting the worst. Ruby motioned would the child like a piece of her banana. For some reason the boy nodded Yes. So he took a piece of banana and ate it. Then he asked for more fruit. "Don't worry about your son," Ruby said. "I have been praying and God has showed me he will be OK."

A woman in the ward heard this and spoke to Ruby. "I have been so ill and prayed constantly to our gods and all they do is taunt me and make fun of me!" There was much anger in her voice. "The true God can heal you," Ruby said. "Do you want me to pray?" "Oh Yes!" "I will ask my husband for a New Testament for you to read about the love of Jesus if you like." So the next day a friend came with the Testament to give to her. She was so happy as Ruby shared with her about the One who cares enough to have given his life for us.

The time came for her and Solomon to take the train back home. By mistake, the one who ordered the ticket got the wrong day—the train leaving just at midnight. He felt so bad. But they went to the station anyway, hoping something could be worked out.

There was a car for invalids on this run. They asked the train guard if they could find a seat now in that car. "You have cancer? I say yes, and your husband too since you need his help." God was opening the way.

As Ruby went to the toilet she looked into the next car. There were two empty seats. "Come, we can sit here!" she exclaimed. Solomon was unsure, since this was a car reserved for women only. But somehow no one objected when they sat down.

As Ruby engaged the woman next to her in conversation, she began to recite all that Jesus was doing for her. The entire car was silent, listening in. Several wanted to have a New Testament to learn about this God who touches his children so tenderly yet so powerfully. So Ruby got to witness to a number of Hindus during the train ride. Hindu gods are demanding and often cruel.

"In all your ways—good and bad—acknowledge Him and He will direct your paths." This is Ruby's way.

Having cancer is not fun.

But Ruby is beaming as she recites her experience. She and Solomon have seen God's hand again and again.

They keep giving thanks in all things.

Two Roads Diverging

In the Hindu world view, all is One. Philosophers call this metaphysical monism of a double kind. All existence is both one in kind and one in number. All distinctions are merely aspects of the One.

As an analogy consider your own person. You are a single human being, not a conglomerate of several humans. Your playful side and your sober side are not two humans that take turns taking over your consciousness. They are two aspects of a single but complex being—namely, yourself.

But eastern world views emphasize the one and downplay the many. They hold that there is one ultimate being—Brahman—a World Soul, if you will. That means that, while Brahman is indescribable in itself, it is helpful for us to think of Brahman as a non-material being, having no size or shape or location. Human souls are understood as Atman. It appears to us that there are many such souls. But in the end all human souls are one soul—Atman. And Atman, in the end, is identical with Brahman. Hence Brahman is the only existing reality.

This is difficult for Westerners to grasp. We tend to think there is a huge multiplicity of things that are distinct—related only by loose external associations.

The task of each human being, according to eastern philosophy, is to return to the One. We live now as fragmented beings, under the illusion that we are separate entities. And that brings suffering to us. Suffering arises when the individual person has desires that conflict with reality. If we could only achieve enlightenment, realizing that all is one, then we would find release from this world of shadows and be lost in the One forever. The World Soul and our soul would be united. Our soul would not exist as such and our sufferings would end.

Each person, then, must work out his own salvation in his own way. All paths of redemption lead to the same destination—the One. When each of us takes a chosen path and follows faithfully, we will arrive at the same End. It is like getting to the top of the mountain by whatever path and then stepping off the summit and vanishing into thin air never to return—thank the gods! Atman in us has been united with Brahman. As separate individuals we are no more.

That explains the caste system. Each soul is struggling on the path of human life because it has not yet gotten to the top. And to come in touch with others who are lower on the path than you only means you go back five spaces. So those who are near the top do not want to touch those below as it means they have to start all over again from the bottom—or at least from a few spaces back. This is why upper caste people are reluctant to mingle with lower caste people.

Jesus taught an entirely different world view. Each soul is a distinct entity created by God that will exist forever. Each person is forever unique. Each is related to God personally.

God, unlike Brahman, knows we are here and cares about us. God is able to give grace to those who want it and ask for it.

Life is like a board game, where the goal is to get to Heaven. When we land on the square of "Salvation" we are allowed to go directly into God's presence, all debts cancelled. No more rolls of the dice are needed.

At that point we do not vanish into thin air. We find ourselves in the midst of a feast ringing with singing and dancing and the joy of relationships—first with our loving heavenly Father and then with each other. This takes place not in some vacuous cloud of nothingness but in a new heaven and new earth like the one we know now—only purged of sin and evil.

This is the meaning of grace—the unmerited favor of a God who loves us and wants us to enjoy His presence forever.

I, for one, am so glad that the ultimate being—God—is not disgusted with me because I am polluted with sin and unfit for his presence. I am so thankful that I do not have come back a million times to work off every sin that stains my soul. He is giving me an extreme makeover fit for His holy presence.

On my faith's board game it says, "Do not pay a fine, Do not pass go again and again, Do not bury yourself in houses and lands. Go directly to the Banquet Hall where the redeemed are celebrating the victory of the Lamb."

Go West, Old Man, Go West

NOVEMBER 15, 2008

"Life's a long journey in the same direction," said some philosopher long ago. And for me, the direction is west.

I had preached my sermon at chapel at New Theological College in India on the day I had to catch the train. I took a chance on the theme "mountains". I had already preached on Bones in the Bible, with some success according to feedback.

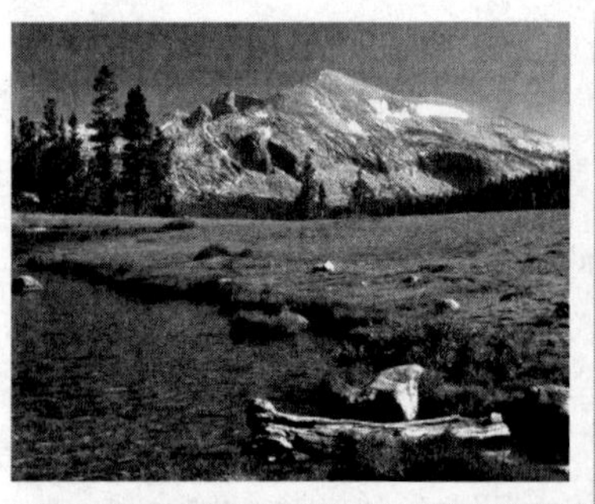

So I took as my text the last chapter of Deuteronomy. As one black pastor put it, Old Man Mose done gone up de mountin'. His eye warn't dim nor his strength abated. And dat is sumpin' given he was 120 at the time.

Mt. Nebo is almost 3000 feet above sea level, right smack dab in front of the lowest lake on earth—the Dead Sea. 100 miles north he could see a white patch—snow-covered Mount Hermon over 9000 feet in elevation. But he could see Mount Tabor, too. He didn't know it at the time, but that's where he and Elijah would come back some 1400 years later to talk with Jesus before Jesus started the last lap of his race with our race.

Moses saw Mount Moriah, where Abraham had won the test of faith when he raised the dreadful knife over Isaac, the son of promise. David would later take the citadel of the Jebusites there and make Jerusalem the forever capital of God's earthly kingdom. And just outside that high place Moses had predicted that a greater prophet than he would come. That prophet would be the lamb that would, unlike Isaac, actually be slain for our redemption.

On the long lonely trek up the trail Moses must have mused on the promise that God would give Abraham a land, a seed, and a blessing for the world. The seed was by now several million souls. They had done well on that part. But they possessed not a single acre of the land. Moses wanted at least to see it before he died. And God had said, OK.

So God took Moses and buried his body somewhere on Nebo—no one knows just where. I think Moses died content. And so may we if we trust God. You see, people don't just croak like frogs. God sends for us—maybe with angels, I don't know. But we don't just die. God takes us. The Bible says, "Precious in the sight of the Lord is the death of his saints."

Meanwhile there's work to be done. Moses perhaps sees the camp of the Israelite hordes a few miles from their first challenge.

Jericho is the first walled city—the oldest one on earth. Ahead were lots of valleys to go through and battles to fight. But as for them, so for us, God is going before. Since Jesus came we know that the land cannot be the geography of Palestine—that's way too small for the billions now in the kingdom. Jesus changed the kingdom from a physical realm to the places where God rules as king. And that is in the hearts of those who like Moses leave the privilege and wealth of the world to seek for the city whose builder and maker is God. Hebrews 11 tells us what we are in for if we join the king—really tough going. But worth every tear shed and drop of blood that we spill in solidarity with the tears, groans and blood of Jesus.

I had a good time preaching all this to those precious brothers and sisters who are going out from college to serve in India, come what may.

One of those is Ashish Kandelwal, whom I met five years ago. He wanted to go into the hills where Christ had never had a presence and start a church. He came to campus the day before I left and told of the school he has now with about 100 kids and several small house churches. Wow!

His wife was a student of mine, too. Preema and Ashish have a year old girl and are just full of joy in the work far off in primitive hill towns a six hour drive from the college. (Preema is no slouch either. She got one of the nation's highest marks in India's national exams as she was finishing New Theological College.)

I thought back on all these blessings as I took the 6-hour train ride through the darkness to Delhi. Upon arrival I wave off the red-turbaned porters eager to carry my luggage. I had no idea where to go if I had used their services. I am waiting for Premji to come into the train to help with my bags. But he doesn't come. I struggle to the platform and sit on a bench. It's midnight. Thankfully there are a few souls nearby, as I have almost no money, no way to call the office, and the platform is not a friendly place to park for long. I keep telling myself he's stuck in traffic. Every five minutes seems like a long time. I keep whistling in the dark, so to speak, to keep up courage. Half an hour later, sure enough, he shows up and we are soon in the little van and off to the airport.

I have five hours to wait. Not enough time to have gone for a hotel room. So I snooze, do Sudoku, and snack on some nuts and an apple I took along. I'm thinking lots of people would think me nuts, floating in a faraway land like that.

But in due time I am on the flight. And—I got an upgrade! Whoo-hoo! One of those larger seats—and by the window. I found out that when you wander to that forward galley usually forbidden to us peons, they have juice and snacks and chips and real fresh fruit that you can just help yourself to! And I do. I never knew how well these wealthy travelers made out. I wonder what its like upstairs in First Class?

I'm by the window, too. I get to see the barren land of Pakistan, Afghanistan, and the other "—stans." I could see tiny squares on the dry hills that marked settlements—far from any roads it seems. Snow-capped ranges in the distance. Beautiful!

But what's this? My seat mate is an Indian who works in London. He tells me he goes back for a month each year to visit family. He thinks India is the most beautiful place on earth. I choose not to challenge that. However, he is antsy. Restless? Man—he was all over, hoggin' the armrests. Jumping in my window seat went I went to the lavatory. Oh well—he was pleasant and I did doze off a dozen times for about ten minutes. After all, I had been up all night.

We flew over the Netherlands. It was fairly clear by then, with the morning sun slanting in under the clouds. We had early morning sun for 8 hours, the pace keeping the full moon on the horizon for hours as we chased it westward. I waved at granddaughter April Gustafson living now in Amsterdam. I doubt she noticed. But it was a nice gesture. I'm all for gestures!

And as I write this at Heathrow Airport in London I have been up nearly 40 hours with a flight across the Atlantic still ahead. I expect Ellie to be at Logan with chauffeur Jim Herrick. She never comes to see me off—only on return. As they say, absence makes the heart grow fonder. Wait 'til I get home from my trip to Kenya next January. She'll probably hire a brass band!

As I sign off the blogs for this excursion of four weeks, I thank everyone for their prayers and thoughts. My heart is full. God, as usual, does wonderful things that make it a joy to venture forth, doing a tiny bit in the sweeping events that will come to a crescendo when the King comes back.

So whether we die on Mt. Nebo or God takes us from our bed in old age, we are the Lord's. Meanwhile—we have work to do, knowing that in the Lord our labor cannot be in vain. You can look it up in I Corinthians 15:58.

The Joy of Giving

I learn so much every time I go to church. And I go often. I follow Jesus and he went every week. I learn something of value each time.

For example, one of the highest aspects of following Jesus is a life of joy.

Now this is not the same as happiness. Happiness depends on things going good for you. Joy can be there even when you are in pain, being rejected, and amidst other kinds of suffering. I talk with people in church every week who have troubles of various sorts but who have an underlying joy.

And remember that religion is mostly about how to escape suffering of various kinds. In fact, one could say that almost all human efforts are directed at keeping suffering at bay. Even boredom is a type of suffering. People chasing good times, playboy escapades, getting money or power or fame comes down to avoiding suffering in its various forms.

Secular people, too, try to have a nice life as long as they can until the grave opens up to swallow them. Religious people try to keep bad karma at bay or to escape the hurly-burly of life through meditation and other techniques. Or they hope to be good enough to earn a good place in the afterlife or maybe buy off the gods.

But Jesus said to the religious people of his time that they had to make God their sole priority, since God does not settle for a mere part of our hearts. Either we love him totally and forsake all else or we are really worshiping gods of our own imagining. This is tough stuff. Most of his followers gave up on him. Why? Because he asks for much more than religious people are willing to give. For example, he tells the guy with money and a good reputation to give it all to the poor and follow him. Of course, the guy doesn't do it. He just cannot be that committed.

We really cannot grasp how radical Jesus' teaching is unless we read the Gospels and the other writings of those who heard him say and do what he said and did. But, amazingly, most who call themselves Christians have not studied the words of this man—the most important single human who ever lived. In fact, most have not even read his teaching even once with an adult mind.

Here's an example of what taking Jesus seriously means.

Today at our church we honored another group of lay people as they launch an effort to help the orphans in Africa. Now these are all lay people who conceived, organized, and are now executing this. They call their group Kulea—an African term for "take care of the children." They formed a non-profit in New Hampshire last December so they can raise money to build orphanages in Tanzania and Kenya.

The HIV-AIDs epidemic has left millions of orphans there. The governments are corrupt and do nothing for them. (Read the latest National Geographic for the plight of women who spend almost all their time fetching water in the drought areas of Kenya and Ethiopia with no help from their government.)

Another example. Last week eight men—mostly electricians—from Common Ground went off to Honduras to build an airstrip for a tribe of 25,000 who have no medical care whatsoever. The goal is to fly in doctors to an abandoned Sandinista era clinic, since there are no roads to these villages. (Common Ground is a fellowship of Christian men from the Merrimack Valley who get together to make a difference where they can.)

Consider these facts.

- One-third of our fellow humans (two billion people) spend all their time trying to get food and water for the day. Among these people 33,000 children die each day from easily preventable diseases due to bad water and sanitation.

- Another two billion are surviving, but on the edge, living on $2 a day on average. A study by researchers showed that women in these areas wanted only two things: their babies to survive and for their kids to have an education—two things we don't even think about for our kids. They know that if their children can read and write they have a chance to use their power to change things. That's why the Taliban, by the way, destroyed hundreds of schools for girls. It is hard to dominate people who can get information. (Even China is having a tough time controlling their people now that the Internet is there.)

- The 48 countries in sub-Saharan Africa have a combined GDP comparable to the city of Chicago. Or put it this way—the combined economies of these 48 nations are less than the assets of the three richest people in the world. (Think Bill Gates, Warren Buffet and some guy from India.)

Now the answer to this, in my view, is not merely political—or even mostly political, even though a key element is corrupt politicians in these nations. Nor is it the United Nations. The main remedy is folks like you and me—as the people starting Kulea—doing what we can directly.

I am a philosophy professor on a pension—not a lot of assets. But I, like you, am among the 1% of the richest people on the planet. One of my greatest joys is going overseas as a volunteer to help educate people in Africa and India and to raise money for other projects like Kulea.

As a follower of Jesus my heart is filled with joy at helping out. Every week I hear about something that makes me reach a little deeper into my wallet. And it is a joy!

But none of this is going to earn me points with God. Reading the writings of St. Paul and St. John I realize that God's love for me is a gift given totally for free. My efforts to make a difference are the result of God's grace, not the cause. Just like my blessing to my grandkids is not given to them because they try to please me so they can earn my love. My blessing is given just because I love them. And that love causes their love to flow back to me. Love like that is unconditional. And it creates love in return because it changes the relationship to one of joy, not one of "I better give a nod to Grandpa or he will cut me out of his will." It's true. It is more fun to give than to receive.

This is why the ideas of Jesus were—and are—so revolutionary. God gave everything to us first. We simply accept it. That changes us so profoundly it is like being born all over again as a different person—a person like Jesus. And that is why giving is for me the greatest joy of all.

Global Village: Living within the Circle of Virtual Grass Huts.

Following a seminar on the Millennial Generation, a bolt of insight struck my brain like lightening out of the mists surrounding the Ivory Tower where this philosophy professor sits. We have now come back to our ancestral tribal villages after centuries of fragmentation.

Picture the typical African village with grass roofed huts and wattle fence. You know everyone in the village and quite a number from villages nearby. You know almost everything about people who live near you—their quirks, their habits, their opinions and talents. In short, the good, the bad and the ugly. In a way, you know more than you need to know or want know. You hear their arguments and the sounds emitting from their huts. Everything seems to hang out in the open.

In York, England, the Yorvik Centre recreates a Viking village of the 10th Century. A man is sitting in an outhouse, screened off by a waist-high fence, all the while conversing with a neighboring housewife a few yards away who is shaking out the thresh in her doorway. Life was very public then, especially compared to a modern home where each person has a private room and maybe a private bath, plus a personal computer, a cell phone, and myriad other gadgets that give control over all unwanted intrusions.

Life for many affluent people today is isolated and hermetically sealed against the natural rhythms of society.

The younger generation, by contrast, is in constant contact with any number of virtual neighbors by texting and social utilities like Facebook, Twitter, and YouTube. The intimate and often embarrassing details of life are now shared with the world. It's a virtual Viking Village or African compound where one knows many titillating details of a person's hopes and dreams, their minds and sometimes their body parts.

This seems to be a new way of overcoming the excessive isolation of their narcissistically inclined parents who insulate themselves behind layers of passwords, caller IDs, and gated villages. But the younger generations are all over Facebook, YouTube, and countless other social networks.

I think we are coming full circle back to the closeness of the ancient villages our ancestors lived in. Only this time we can choose which village to live in, simply by being selective about the networks we sign on for. We can admit new people to our village any time we choose. And we can marginalize or de-select those whom we find obnoxious.

Christianity—or Jesus?

Jesus stands as the unique figure in all of history, fulfilling the ideals of both religion and philosophy.

It may sound arrogant to say this but I believe it to be true, nonetheless, and ask you to hear me out with an open mind and heart. If at the end of this you decide I am blind, narrow-minded and ignorant, then I'll not object if you consign me to intellectual outer darkness, where there is, no doubt, weeping and gnashing of teeth as they used to say.

What I am about to say is not original. Others have made the same claim in various ways. I hope to induce you to consider who Jesus is as he is presented in the original presentations of his life and teaching by those who were close to him.

First, Jesus did not come to start a religion. He was born into a religious community and he never rejected his spiritual heritage. He did correct and purify and enlarge upon that heritage, as his contemporaries understood it. As he put it, he did not come to destroy the Law and the Prophets of the Jewish Bible, but to fulfill them.

The uniqueness of Jesus' teaching is the distinction between relationship and religion. A direct relationship with the one and only God is everything. Religion without such a relationship is nothing.

Religion is man's attempt to relate to the Ultimate Reality in which we live. That Reality has been conceived in a variety of ways, some more religious and some more philosophical. The religion is to enable human beings by their own efforts to nto a reality that is larger and more powerful and enduring an us in order to fulfill what it means to be human. Everyone grees that we came from some ancient origin. We did not create ourselves. Something or someone else brought humans into being.

Religion, broadly speaking, tells us what we should do in order to secure whatever peace or power we need to maximize our existence. The main idea is basically this. "Do this and you will live a satisfying and flourishing life."

Jesus contradicts this. Life is not what we do. It is not an achievement of our own will or intellect.

Rather, he said, it is embracing what has been done not *by us* but *for us* by connecting with the Person who has already accomplished all that is needed for us to enjoy a satisfying and flourishing life.

We do not strive to achieve a relationship with God. We accept God's offer to have a relationship with us. God has done it all. We embrace what God is willing to give us. God offers an invitation; we accept it. It's like any friendship. You cannot earn a friendship. You cannot buy a friendship. Friendship is always a gift another person freely gives you.

Religion advises us on how to make our selves presentable to God or to the Ultimate Reality as each world view understands it. Accept these doctrines. Do these good deeds. Train yourself to be a noble person of virtue. Then you will be rewarded with the fruits of your efforts—Heaven, or Paradise, or Nirvana. Jesus says that all of this is fruitless because what is required for salvation (a satisfying and flourishing life both here and hereafter) cannot be achieved in this way. Human effort cannot provide what we need.

All that is needed for our salvation (a satisfying and flourishing life) has been provided by God himself and is a gift to us provided we choose to receive it.

We must do something. But what we must do is not to participate in building our salvation but to accept it as offered to us. That requires us to completely change our minds, our direction. Instead of justifying myself as a sincerely good person (with faults and mistakes, to be sure) who is trying to be good enough to achieve salvation, I must admit my helplessness and own up to my sins against God, throwing myself upon God's mercy and grace.

In other words, I give myself up to God. I admit that I have not loved God with all my being. I see that I have focused on myself—on what I want, rather than on the God who gives me life and offers me salvation. This twisting of the soul has resulted in my loving things and formulating dreams that I think will help me achieve a satisfying and flourishing life according to my own notions. This is at the root of what induces me to deceive myself, to hurt other people, and in the end to ruin myself.

Jesus says that forgiveness and healing come only as gifts received in a relationship with God—the one who loves us and gave himself for us. "For the *gift* of God is eternal life, through Jesus Christ our Lord." (Romans 6:23) "It is not because of works of righteousness that we have done, but in virtue of his mercy that God saves us." (Titus 3:5) "It is the gift of God, not because of works, that none should boast in God's presence." (Ephesians 2: 8-9)

There is no religion or philosophy that speaks like this. Jesus' message is unique. He alone claimed to be the Infinite-personal Creator come to Earth to do for us what we could never do for ourselves. He then offers his accomplishment as a gift to any who will forsake their self-designed plans for a satisfying and flourishing life and give themselves wholly to the One who came to save us. "While we were still sinners, Christ died for us." (Romans 5:8)

There are dozens of passages in the writings about Jesus that say this. You could do an Internet search yourself.

By contrast, consider other views on how one can achieve a flourishing and satisfying life.

1. Secular humanism (or philosophical naturalism) teaches that you are on your own. There is no God or spiritual entity to provide salvation or advice or hope. Others have written their viewpoints, but they are merely human ideas in the end. Therefore you must do what you think is best with the short time you have in life. When you die, that's it. Your person is extinguished—forever gone. A good life is up to you and you alone.

2. Eastern religions have many variations but agree on something like this. You are in a cycle of incarnations that will carry your soul through many experiences. Each incarnation is another round of suffering for failures of a previous life. You must accept your duty to live in such a way as to build up good karma so that you will rise eventually to a point of release and not return to this world again. Your soul will then achieve

nirvana and you will lose individual consciousness by being absorbed into the ultimate One. It's up to you to save yourself by selfless effort until your individual existence ceases.

3. Monotheistic religions.

   a. Judaism advises you to live by the Tanack given by God's prophets so that you will be admitted to the realm of the just. Worship God and do the good deeds he requires and heaven will be your reward when you die.

   b. Christianity is often portrayed as a religion in which we do our best to love God and be good to others with a sincere heart. Believe that Jesus died for your sins and mistakes and you will probably go to heaven to live with God, if your good deeds show you are sincere.

   c. Islam requires that you sincerely confess that there is no God but Allah and that Muhammad is his prophet. Submit to the requirements of the Koran in which Allah shows his will. Allah knows you are weak. He is merciful. If your good deeds outweigh your bad deeds, you will enjoy the virgins of Paradise (unless Allah decrees otherwise, for Allah can do whatever he wants with you no matter what you have achieved.) Allah, being incomprehensibly lofty, does not relate personally with you as a friend, but he provides a place for you to experience happiness.

4. The Way of Jesus. You have already offended a God so holy he cannot tolerate any sin whatever—not even one. You sin because you are sinful. You are therefore doomed—without God and without hope. Nothing you do can make yourself eligible for salvation. But—Good News! God loves you and wants you to be in personal direct relationship with Him. He has provided salvation without your help. Admit you have no chance of fixing yourself. Accept the free gift of salvation provided through the life, death, and resurrection of Jesus. Turn your life entirely over to God through Jesus and God will accept you into his family. He will fill you with his own life. You will follow Jesus in everything you do. You will have joy and peace, eagerly doing anything to serve God every day—not out of fear you may be rejected, but out of love for the God who has rescued you and adopted you forever.

The stark contrast between the Way of Jesus and the religions of mankind comes down to two words: Do or Done! Religions say Do this or that. Jesus says everything is all done already.

This is unique—one of a kind. Jesus is either Lord (as he claimed) or a deluded fanatic or a lying charlatan. He is not merely another good moral teacher advising us what to do to achieve the ultimate flourishing life. As C. S. Lewis said, Jesus did not leave us that option—he did not intend to leave us that option.

Let me end with an analogy.

I once set my hopes on getting into Heavenly Timeshares. The description of this place was exactly what I wanted. If I could just go there everything I truly longed for would be mine. I knew that you had to live up to high standards. Not just anyone was admitted.

I would have to learn about the life of the Founder—his mission to reach people who suffer a lot and have little or nothing. I thought he was the most wonderful person who ever lived. I wanted to be like him. So I started imitating his lifestyle. I knew it was way above my ability. But if I tried hard I thought maybe I would be accepted. I knew Heavenly Timeshares was expensive. That was understandable, for the best always costs a lot. So I started an account to put in everything I could—money, time, even prayer. Maybe I wasn't Mother Teresa, but I was going for it as best I could.

After many years of my best effort I talked with a representative of Heavenly Timeshares, telling him all that I was doing. I was making constant deposits in the Good Deeds account. I was gathering endorsements from references that I thought would put in a good word for me when it was time for my Final Interview.

What the rep told me was such a SHOCK!

"Hey, man, you are already in! They are putting the finishing touches on your Timeshare now. The Owner says he knows you and you are one of his relatives—a brother I think he said. It's all settled. So Heavenly Timeshares appreciates all you are contributing—that really helps our mission. But as for you—you are all set. It doesn't get any better than to be on the Friends and Family list! And actually, you may not know this, but everyone in Heavenly Timeshares has to be on the Friends and Family list. That's the only way in. Congratulations!"

Darwin Is Dead—Long Live Darwin

THE DEATH OF THE DARWINIAN DINOSAUR

It finally became clear to me that Darwin is essentially dead. Rather, Darwinism is dead—or at most on life support. It has become an intellectual fossil to be displayed among paradigms and theories that once were powerful but have lost their explanatory power. Like most ageing religions, it still has its promoters. But the end is near.

Let me explain.

For years I have presented to my philosophy students the options available to explain the universe and our place in it. One of the big questions debated has been between chance and design. Is the universe a teleological system or a-teleological? That's is, has an intelligence created the universe for some purpose? Or is it just something that happened on its own and is unguided, thus having no purpose as such?

I have always presented the supporting arguments for both sides as convincingly as possible. And I have often stepped into the world of naturalism and sat in Darwin's chair in order to see reality from his perspective. Over time the view from that chair has become less and less enchanting.

I was watching a football game when this moment of clarity came to me. It occurred to me that the struggle between the two opposing sides, intelligent design and pure chance, is a bit like a football game, with each team trying to finish off the other. Who will win? Will it be the naturalist team—*The Dinosaurs*— with Darwin at quarterback calling plays and the agnostic linemen blocking for atheist running backs? Or will it be the *Grand Design* team with players like William Paley, William Dembski, Michael Behe and Francis Collins?

On TV today the New England Patriots have a 20-10 lead and are running down the clock with under two minutes to go. There is a mathematical possibility that the Carolina Panthers could recover a fumble, score a touchdown, do an onside kick and make a 60-yard field goal to send the game into overtime. But realistically, the game is over. The Patriots have the ball. The outcome is decided.

The same holds for this philosophical debate. The two-minute warning has been given now. *Grand Design* has just taken the lead and has possession of the ball. I think the game is over. The *Darwin Dinosaurs* are done; *Grand Design* has won. Evolutionism is still on the field but is essentially defeated.

Darwin's bulldogs are getting more desperate and shrill. The Design team is now capturing the majority of fans.

How has this happened?

For over a century the *Darwin Dinosaurs* built a winning franchise. The fossil records, with a little bit of tweaking that the referees never noticed, seemed to show the progress of complexity over millions of years. One could then assume that the picks of geologists would soon unearth the missing links. Everything would be explained without appealing to a design factor.

Then came microbiology, examining human cells. Darwin knew nothing of the cell's composition—it was blob of gelatin for all he knew over 150 years ago. Now we know a lot. What is contained in a single cell is an incredible complexity of wonders that stretches Darwinian assumptions to the breaking point. It now takes a huge *leap of faith* to believe that chance could create this complexity in a few hundred million years. It is the Darwinists who embrace blind faith. To see the hand of intelligence in it is now a small and logical step.

What is lighting the fuses of militant Darwinian fans like Richard Dawkins?

Desperation perhaps? It is a shame to see scientists of his caliber, who are theoretically committed to follow evidence wherever it leads, resort to rhetorical tricks that shows desperation. They seem to be hoping for a Hail Mary long-ball. Umm— make that a Hail Darwin.

Meanwhile Francis Collins, Michael Behe, William Dembski, Phillip Johnson, Hugh Ross and many others argue for an over arching intelligence as the only adequate explanation for the complexity of the universe as we know it. Even one of atheism's most prestigious voices has switched sides, now concluding there is a deistic Intelligence that authored the complex universe we live in. He is Antony Flew.

Intelligence is at work. Chance operating over time cannot explain what is now before our wondering eyes. Is that intelligence the God of Genesis? Or the god of Aristotle who operates internally within the universe? The most sophisticated candidate is the God whom Jesus Christ revealed in his matchless teachings. But the point is this—there is an intelligence at work in all that has unfolded since the Big Bang some 13 billion years ago.

Admittedly, looking at the issue from the perspective of a cosmologist we cannot prove that the intelligent creator reveals himself in sacred documents or has visited planet Earth in person as Christians believe. But it makes such claims conceivable.

Another problem with Darwinism—and to some extent Intelligent Design—is that they operate within the paradigm of Cartesian foundationalism—the attempt to prove the absolute truth of a set of abstract ideas about Reality that give a cogent and coherent account of what C. S. Lewis called "the Whole Show." This paradigm is losing credit among philosophers.

So the crux of the concern is shifting to a focus on the value and meaning of human life rather than speculation about the nature of existence as a whole. While a world view must accommodate a reasonable explanation of scientific facts as we currently know them, it must also be practical—a world view that enhances life—in which life can flourish.

Here Darwinism is at a second disadvantage. If humans are no more than intelligent animals what can one aspire to? While it may be theoretically possible for us to create a world of peace and prosperity, the odds are against it. Human beings tend to be self-centered. If one believes that death is the end of one's existence forever, why fight against the dark side of human nature? Why be concerned for the health of the planet since biology claims that every species goes extinct sooner or later anyway.

Even if one enjoys a life of ease there is a spiritual hunger in us that yearns for transcendence. I suppose education could possibly erase this aspect of our nature. That would prove difficult. Furthermore, would it be desirable even it could be done?

What is the likelihood that social engineering of the human person would result in harmony and a flourishing culture? Wherever social engineering has been tried on a large scale it has not made things better. Social engineering on a large scale proved disastrous in Germany and later in Communist countries.

What makes us better is a commitment to a higher cause, especially a transcendent cause. It takes a renovation of the heart that inspires us to serve a transcendent meta-narrative. Darwinism is unable to support such a commitment. A teleological view of the universe can sustain it. There is a Grand Design that beckons us. If the evidence points to an Intelligence that is pulling the universe toward a transcendent end, our task is to seek a relationship with this Intelligence that will satisfy the innate longings of the human heart. That intelligence has spoken through the genetic code in a convincing way. Has that Intelligence spoken to us more directly in human language? Maybe if we seek, we will find the answer.

Famous Last Chapter

The purpose of this reflection on the last chapter in the Gospel of Matthew is to tease out of the literature insightful nuggets of understanding. Eventually each of us will have a last chapter spoken or written about us. While we should never put a period down when the sentence of our lives is still going forward, we can get a lot out of pondering what others have written about the last chapter of the lives of notable people or of fictional characters.

Let's start with the last chapter of the Gospel that Matthew wrote centuries ago.

Matthew 28 The time: after the Sabbath.

In Jewish history the Sabbath day is the last day of the week, on which God is pictured as taking joyful pleasure in the artistry of his creation. "It was very good." "This is Great!" God said this after creating a human being, the crown of his work.

While often called a day of rest, it cannot be so literally, since an infinite Being never needs rest in the sense that we mortals do. For us, it is a day, not of inactivity, but of different activity. Neither God nor we are capable of doing nothing. Arduous labor, by which we wrest a living from the earth by the sweat of the brow, is set aside so that we can re-create our soul's need to enjoy what God has done in us and in nature. As Bob Sabean has put it, it is a day of re-creation—a day to renew our relationship with our Creator and our bonds with other people.

What a shame to define it as a day of somber soul-searching and deadening negatives. Basically what God did and invites us to join in is something like this: Enjoy!

But for the women of this chapter the Sabbath is over. The workweek has begun. One must get a jump on the day in order not to fall behind. Life has many demands.

For us who know God and love God any day elicits a cheerful "Good morning, Lord—what are your assignments for me today? I want to be effective in the things of the kingdom, the things that truly matter."

He assigns us the job of doing our work as part of His work, no matter how difficult, unpleasant, arduous it may at times be. We follow God's example. In Jesus he poured himself out for us through much suffering and even death.

For the women here mentioned the prospects are unpleasant. The week is not off to a good start.

Arising before first light, they gather the materials for their grim task and set off on the familiar path to the tombs. They have been here and done that before. They can walk this familiar trail even in darkness. They are silent, each alone with her thoughts, going over once again what they have endlessly rehearsed in a nearly sleepless night—the spirit-crushing events of the tragedy. Their Jesus—master yet friend—has passed through his trial, his agony, his taunting and his death. The taunting echoes in their minds. "He claimed to save others—why doesn't he save himself?" "If God favors him, let God rescue him!"

Why couldn't they just kill him and be done with it? Why had they spewed such venom into his failing ears. Forsaken by his disciples—even by the Father He had revealed to them. By them all—except for John and themselves, who were with Him to the end. There, when they pulled the spikes out of his limbs to be used to pin another criminal to a cross. There, when Joseph and Nicodemus carried the body to a nearby tomb. There, when they covered him with a shroud and sealed the stone after it thudded into place.

Today is the first day of a bleak week. God had assigned them a task and they would see it through—two of them called Mary, but not Mary the mother of Jesus from Nazareth. She had been at her son's death and was not to be expected to do this dismal service.

So for us, when we feel least up to the task, we still must serve our Jesus. We may not know what sense our efforts make. But God knows. That is enough. "Go—just go. You! Go as they did, even to your rendezvous with hopelessness. Even to look at whatever grave gapes before you."

Then—it happens! God lights the fuse of his pyrotechnics. This was planned in the counsels of eternity before time began. God would show up in glory and power. In this case an earthquake as unseen tectonic plates deep in the bowels of Earth shrug, releasing tension building up for decades.

At this very hour, when his chosen precious ones are at the low tide of life, God thunders forth his presence, almighty to save. He sets the prisoner free from terror and grief. A tidal wave is about to curl upon the dry shoreline of faith.

Through an angel—those messengers of fire and fury—God rolls the stone from the tomb where Satan, the Accuser of God's children, has bound the Strong One, the champion of heaven, the David who came to defeat Goliath. The stone that supposedly sealed Jesus' doom now proves the accuracy of God's sling. Death itself is now dead, never again to terrorize those who walk in its shadow.

The angel sits upon the stone, in utter disdain for the devil's brief triumph. The One in whom we set our hopes is no longer there. The tomb is empty! Now the tomb of the shattered heart will begin to fill with Light from heaven, yes, with the Water of Life.

His clothing is light itself, his appearance like lightening. "So God imparts to human hearts the blessings of His heaven."

What has become of the hapless guards hired to make sure none of this would happen? How the strong ones quake. How the mighty are fallen. They may as well be dead. The hirelings of the Accuser cannot prevail when God shows up in power. They will later collect their wages—bribes to seal lips of those sent to guard the seal on the mouth of the tomb. Bribes against the truth of what happened to them when their strength became as water poured on the ground. But for now, they are as useless as infants, as feeble as they are frail.

"I will fear no evil, for thou art with me. Thy rod and thy staff, they comfort me." These holy phrases from the Psalms will have new meaning for these women, now in shock, speechless.

Only the angel can speak. What wonderful words—words longed for but that none dared hope for. For all hope was gone.

"Fear not! Do not be afraid."

Not afraid? With earthquakes and paralyzed soldiers, and a Messenger so dazzling it's like looking into the noonday sun?

"I know you are looking for Jesus—the One who was crucified."

Even now, whether we are aware of it or not, we are all looking for Jesus, for Yeshua—the God who saves.

Life is brutal without Him. Or at least it rings hollow. Even in the exotic pleasures the world proffers, the laughter echoes down a cavern of despair.

We cannot get out of life alive—and we know it.

Sometimes it is hard even to be alive while our lungs are still breathing air. Are we being crucified by degrees each day, yet without the drops of blood that should alarm us of our peril?

But the One we seek is not here in our silent catacombs. He is not in our halls of learning, our salons of pleasure, or our arenas of passion.

Yet the angel knows what we are looking for and God has sent his messenger to help us. God knew where the women would be drawn—to the last vestige of the one they loved, now decaying in a borrowed crypt. They have come to do what they can—to prepare the remains for permanent burial, much as we bury hopes that can never be. We know things can never be the same when our world goes to pieces. How can we just sweep up the pieces into a tidy pile and then just go on with life?

The angel's message? "He is risen!" What can that mean? They see the evidence—his body is no longer on the cold stone shelf, waiting to be perfumed against the stench of death. Why are they surprised? Jesus had told them he would raise up the temple—the temple of his body where God had come to dwell, a temple of the spirit not of stone. Not that they had grasped his intent....

He is living now in a new dimension of reality. This world is but a creaking shadow of that new heaven and earth—the kingly rule of God. The women have no time to process this astounding revelation, to make sense out of what is assaulting their minds.

Though they understand nothing they have seen and heard something extraordinary. They are sent immediately to pass the word along to the rest of the disciples. The Twelve should report back to Galilee where everything had begun. To the lake where a carpenter turned rabbi had summoned them, "Follow me and I will make you fishers of men."

"Now I have told you!" the angel declares. That's all there is for now. No full explanation of the future program. No Q & A session. That's it. Take the next step. It's now up to you.

So the women hurry off to find the cowering men.

Once again Jesus has countered the culture. Women are entrusted with this message first—in a culture where the testimony of women counted for nothing. No wonder they are afraid yet filled with joy. Such emotions are not always contradictory.

The man they meet on the way is not the one they expected.

"Greetings!"

A single word changes their lives and the life of all humanity forever. It is not so much the word as the One who utters it. With what tone of voice did it come to their ears? Authority yet warmth, one supposes. Startling yet tender.

Only one response is possible. They must touch him, not as Thomas would a week later, to assure their doubts. Theirs is not an analytical response of the mind but one of the heart.

At his feet they fall in worship. Yet they touch him, not to reassure but in an embrace of love. God has come to them, to women. Perhaps they, unlike the chosen Twelve, had listened to his conversations over the last months and grasped, as the men did not, what Jesus said of himself. He was the Son of the Most High. He is One whom even a Jew can worship.

Having been sent to the disciples by the angel, the women repeat Jesus' instructions. Tell them we shall rendezvous in Galilee.

By now the guards have shaken off their paralysis and made their way back to headquarters. What were they to say? No denial is possible since all know the tomb was sealed to prevent intrusion from the outside. Now it was empty, the result of an inside job admitting of no cover-up.

Can you hear the sergeant speaking? "You are never going to believe this, but...." Death would be the expected penalty. But then who would vouch for the cover-up the chief priests agreed upon after a brief conference? "Say you fell asleep and when you awoke the body was gone. Everyone knows guards often sleep on duty. If the Romans hear of it we'll cover for you. Take some money, do as we say, and shut up." Their fabrication was widely believed for many a year.

As a result Jerusalem does not know the reality. As at his birth, the glory of the redeeming God is hidden from the self-appointed big people and revealed to the nobodies no one takes note of. Jesus appears in Galilee—a region from which nothing good can be expected. It is where Jesus plied his trade as an artisan in earlier years after the death of Joseph, his earthly father. Here he had provided for the family who likely lived on a small plot of land farmed on a subsistence basis while he took carpentry work in nearby villages, including perhaps Sepphoris, a Roman settlement. Here he did the odd job for fishing families at the lake. Perhaps he had worked on the boats from which he preached to the crowds and in which he crossed to the other side. Here he had called his first disciples, fed the multitudes, and healed Peter's mother-in-law.

Here he had rolled out the kingdom message—the Sermon on the Mount. Somewhere on that same upland he would now meet those who had walked with him through thick and thin and would soon take the Good News to all the earth.

When they saw Jesus they too worshiped him. Once he was to them a rabbi who spoke as no one had ever spoken. Rather than taking them on as learners to groom them for the established religious order, Jesus had begun to break down the barriers they all took for granted. He taught women. He honored the poor and chastised the wealthy. He reached out to despised Samaritans and even Gentiles.

Now he had conquered the last enemy—death. Yet some, the text says, doubted. How can it be that we can doubt what is before our own eyes? Such is the confusion of the human condition that we sometimes cannot settle on what seems incomprehensible. But then the Holy Spirit—God—would soon indwell them, enabling them to do the impossible, even to the point of death.

Now he would commission them to extend this kingdom of God that makes no distinction on the basis of race, gender, or economic condition.

"Go into all the world," commands this one who now has all authority in heaven and earth. "Make disciples, baptizing them into a new life, a new order of existence in the name of the triune God."

They would soon make disciples just as Jesus had discipled them, ready to obey all he had commanded them.

He promised to be with them always, even to the very end of this world as we know it.

And Jesus has kept his word.

Hey Seuss!

An interview with Jesus (rhymes with *Dr. Seuss—think Spanish pronunciation*) Godman

CHAT ONE

Hey, Seuss! What's up?

Godman: You know I don't like you messing around with my name like that. Why can't you show some respect and stick with Godman?

OK, God. Sorry—I can't help it—you have such a weird Hispanic-sounding name.

Godman: You still with that self-awareness group? Aren't you getting tired?

What you mean: "tired?"

Godman: Tired of playing god – guide yourself, forgive yourself, plan all, do all, decide all?

Well, frankly, it is growing a bit thin—and not doing much for me when I stop to think about it—which isn't often. But what's the alternative?

Godman: First step: deal with your sins.

How often do I sin, anyway? I'm a nice person.

Godman: You must love others as you love yourself. Monitor that for just one day, OK?

What counts as a sin—other than the obvious, like killing someone or rape or stealing and lying?

Godman: It all starts with your mind - what kind of thoughts. You give yourself breaks all the time. You know - "I was tired or had a bad day or was in pain - that's why I snapped at him or said that cutting comment to her...." Do you give others the same breaks?

Geez no! I cannot drive downtown without thinking "he's a bad driver, she's probably a tramp or they obviously are creeps."

Godman: You don't pray for these people. You don't make allowances for them, thinking they might have just gotten news a family member has cancer or he may have gotten divorce papers in the day's mail or she may be wracked with back pain?

No, you're right—that never enters my mind in most cases.

Godman: Well—that's all sin and has to be confessed.

Really! It's gonna take a long time in my case. It'll never happen—a complete catalog...?

Godman: Not to worry, there's a package deal.

Whazzat?

Godman: Just confess your sins in thought word and deed all the time— because you are not just one who does sins but you are a sinner—it flows out of you as easy as water from a spring because that's what you are.

I don't like the word sin, to be truthful. Makes me feel like I should feel guilty. I'm just a good person who makes mistakes once in a while—like every one else. I'm not perfect—but I'm not a bad person.

Godman: You remember Jim, right? He couldn't believe he had cancer – he felt super! But it was there and would've killed him but for the operation. It didn't matter that he looked healthier than most guys 10 years younger and didn't think he had any symptoms to put him in the "I have a fatal disease" category.

So you think I have soul cancer...?

Godman: Exactly. You are a person with cancer of the heart and it will kill you if you don't admit it and take action. Sin has metastasized throughout your being. But there's one way you can become a survivor.

Only one way, huh? And you have the answer, eh?

Godman: "Eh, Seuss," you mean—be serious for once will you?

Sorry. What are you getting at?

Godman: Admit yourself to God's cancer clinic and let God apply the only cure there is.

What's that mean? I don't like hospitals and doctors—they put you under, do to you what THEY think is right, and you either come out alive or you don't. Either they fix it or you come out botched up. Scares me!

Godman: What's your alternative? Doctor yourself, right? You know that's not going to work.

OK – but there are lots of cures out there that are in the "we'll fix you if you do what we say" business! And I know you're not talking about some trip to Mexico for a quick and painless stay at an alternative therapy, right?

Godman: You know what has to happen. You go for radical surgery with a life-long follow-up regimen. No other way.

That's so, like, demanding. Why change my whole life with something so total when I'm not sure it'll be right for me? Who's to say there's only one religion that can cure?

Godman: Look at the track record! What's the morbidity rate? Beside, we're not talking religion here—that's man's attempts to find a cure for himself by the 12 step this or the 8-fold that. I'm talking about the God who made you, who knows all about you, who cares about you—and who has not yet lost a person who comes under his care and follows through on the prescriptions.

Not even one? Come on! That's a stretch, the way I look at it.

Godman: OK. You come back tomorrow and we'll explore that?

Sure. Why not? See you then, Godman. Thanks for the time.

CHAT TWO

Hey, Seuss! Er.... hey, Godman!

Godman: Hello, my friend. Great day, isn't it?

Not so sure – I've been troubled by what we talked about the other day.

Godman: Why is that?

It's all your fault. All I could think of was how many times I had rotten thoughts about people—some I haven't even met—all the while excusing myself for all kinds of things I do that aren't quite right!

Godman: "Love others as you love yourself." You can't do it even for one day.

A day? Not for an hour—unless I'm asleep. And even that is not always pretty!

Godman: Now we're making progress! You know why you can't do it? You can't love God the way you should, so you can't love your neighbor.

I don't follow....

Godman: It's simple. You were made by God to run on the fuel of the Holy Spirit. God is to be the center of life, holding everything together like a hub holds the spokes that keep the wheel perfectly round so it can roll smoothly down the road of life. You would rather do it your own way, so you pushed God to the edges and took over. That's the original sin that leads to all the others. You do not—you cannot—love God with all your heart, soul, mind and strength.

No denying that one. I'll concede that much. But that's a high bar no one can vault over. Shees! Loving God totally all the time. You gotta be kidding!

Godman: Think of it this way. You want to get to another planet and back? You've no margin for mistakes. Zero tolerance for screw-ups, right?

Well, duh! One error and you ain't comin' back. That's been proved.

Godman: It has to be perfect. And the same is true for the soul.

Ahhhhh.... Take that apart for me?

Godman: Sure. Your attempts to fix things that need fixing are not going to work. God knows that. Name any religion you want. Or secularism. Or any "you-name-it" theory about how to have a good life. It never works.

Why is that?

Godman: Because you either ignore the symptoms, minimizing the problem or you fool yourself into thinking you can figure it out for yourself, do it your way, and come out OK when all is said and done. Failure rate on this track is 100% It's never because of works that you come up with. You are without God and thus without hope in the world.

So we're doomed if we do and doomed if we don't.

Godman: No way! Put God back into the center and he can fix the mess and see that you land safely in the next world.

Really! How can you say that?

Godman: I didn't say it. God says it. He came to rescue you. He will do a heart transplant. He has your blood type, so when his life comes into your life stream it will purge you of all the spiritual toxins and result in life with him forever.

But what about those sins I do every day—and the guilt?

Godman: The guilt is gone because God took them all out when you went under for the surgery. There are still some sin cells here and there but in time they will do less damage and eventually be eradicated completely. That's when life begins. And meanwhile you have the joy of knowing the One who created you is fixing you. When he's done and the stitches heal, you'll never show signs of how ugly you used to be when sin disfigured you.

I think I read you. Maybe I'm ready for some time on my knees.

Jane

I have a friend who grew up in the church. Let's call her Jane. Jane's parents attended faithfully when she was a girl. Well – mostly her mother.

Jane attended Sunday school and youth group and to this day says she believes in God. On everything else she is mushy. Going off to worship God with others is not thought necessary. She has young grandchildren now.

"Won't I go to heaven?" is her question.

I am not the one to answer that question. God makes that call, not me.

But she presses me—seeking some assurance. For some reason there seems to be something niggling in her mind. What shall I reply?

Perhaps I'll tell her to read what Jesus has to say about this. Since she considers herself a Christian.

What will Jesus say?

As I understand it, she will not get comforting re-assurance.

Everyone Jesus spoke to in his ministry believed in God. But he said that few of them would be saved. Unlike Jane, they all went to worship God in their houses of worship every week and attended festivals in addition. So I guess their commitment was stronger than hers.

But Jane thinks she is a good person. And she is. No one could dispute that. But is that the admission ticket for heaven?

According to Jesus, the answer is a definite no.

Jane prays. Isn't that enough? Again, no.

The requirement Jesus makes in bright bold colors is this. One turns around one's life by repenting of its self-direction.

You see, Jane appears to be where we all start out. Embracing her own idea of what God is or should be like rather than submitting to what God has shown us in Jesus. She has to throw all that away as rubbish.

Jane wants to have heaven on her own terms. Just be a good person, have nice thoughts about God, respect Jesus, help other people, and you'll be in.

But heaven is God's and Jesus is the gatekeeper. He sets the entrance requirements and we either take it or leave it. We are not in a position to modify it.

The requirements start with giving up control over your own life 100% in order to live out God's will not your own. Jane has never done this.

Even those who are doing this find it a tough discipline to implement every day. But that is the deal. Jesus will give his life 100% to you if you give yours 100% to him.

So if Jane wants to do this, what will her life look like?

Will she have to attend worship meetings and take part in group events with other followers of Jesus?

This is a bizarre question.

Let's use an analogy.

Jane is a wife and a grandmother. Does she have to care for her husband every day and go visit the grandchildren when the family is celebrating their birthdays?

A strange question isn't it?

If Jane asks this question she may be a nominal member of the family but she is not a vital member of it. If she were, her heart would never think like that. A genuine wife and mother would be so committed that she would be thinking all the time of how she can maximize her time with the ones she loves. And should that love falter, Jane would be concerned about that coolness—deeply troubled—and would do everything she could think of to repair the relationship so the love could flow freely.

So when Jane says she can follow God at home alone, she doesn't get it.

Jesus insisted we love God and his people with a fervent love that impels us to be connected passionately with God and his people. If God has our hearts then we will be thinking all the time of how we can draw close to Him, how we can help in what God is trying to do in the world, and how we can be with the family of God as much as possible.

When Jane asks how much she must give of herself she shows that she does not love God with all her heart, soul, mind and strength nor her neighbor as herself.

But that, Jesus insists, is the bottom line commitment. Without that, no matter how much Jane thinks she is OK with God, she is not. She is in a false position and totally deceived as to her hopes for heaven. She is exactly where God's great Enemy wants her to be. The road she is on is not the one to heaven at all. Jane is on the broad road. We know where that one ends up.

Jane needs to get off at the nearest exit and change directions.

Jane needs a heart transplant, not a few heartburn pills.

Jane needs to realize that she is making a god she feels comfortable with but who cannot save her. According to Jesus, Jane is lost despite her Christian sentiments.

Of course, maybe Jesus did not know what he was talking about. Jane needs to search Jesus' message as though her life depends on it.

Because it does.

God's Football League

Following Jesus is a team sport. He is our coach, calling the plays.

He is the greatest player ever. No fumbles, no interceptions, no missed field goal attempts. He overcame injuries that threatened to take him down for good.

His league now has many franchises—all over the world. Teams have different uniforms and mascots. But they all claim to play for Jesus. Some are doing well, some not.

How is your team doing?

Some teams are still deep in their own territory where the opposition has them backed up to their own end zone. The team is not getting along even with each other. They cannot agree on what play to call. Some are changing the playbook. Working at cross-purposes they are now 4th and long and may go down to defeat. The *Red Devils* are pushing them toward defeat. Many such teams have had their franchise closed down or sold off.

Maybe your team is near mid-field but not going anywhere. You have a few good plays. But some on the team are more interested in grabbing headlines for themselves than sacrificing for team yardage. As said, it is a team sport and Jesus calls the plays. This is not golf where you get to play the ball as you see fit.

Hopefully your team is marching down field. Maybe in the Red Zone already. Perhaps you have scored points and are facing the 4th Quarter with confidence. You have memorized the playbook.

You execute in sync with others on the team. You play for Jesus, whether the press notices you or not.

Not a lot of time on the clock? Just about out of time-outs? Get in the huddle and review the playbook. Then execute with all you've got in the position you have been given. If a lineman, block. If in the secondary, tackle. If a halfback, run. If a receiver, catch. A quarterback? Throw.

Are you in the game or on the bench? Or perhaps just in the stands. The playoffs are coming. Then it will be over.

A victory parade, or a rout? Which will it be?

Where Christianity Got into Trouble

Even though I am a follower of Jesus, I think that his followers have gotten off track from time to time.

Digging into the world system is what I call it.

Jesus told his followers that his kingdom was not of this world—the visible world we all know from birth and study through science and history. The leaders of the nations and tribes all focus on the power and control they can grab in an effort to achieve glory, fame, and especially stuff.

Jesus said his kingdom was not in the visible world. It is a heavenly kingdom. This heavenly kingdom will one day absorb and transcend the world of here and now. But God will bring that about, not humans.

Jesus predicted the destruction of the Jewish Temple that was the pride and joy of that people. And he taught that all the things we are so proud of in this world will melt into nothingness some day.

Jesus' kingdom is in the hearts of those who love God as Jesus revealed him.

When they came to lynch him, Jesus forbade his guys to fight to save him. In fact he insisted they love their enemies—and he set the example. He prayed that God would forgive those who were torturing and killing him.

So whenever Jesus' people use the methods of this world system to advance Jesus' kingdom they are on the wrong track.

The Jewish Temple in Jerusalem was the pride and joy of Israel. (The Muslim mosque, the Dome of the Rock is now on that site.) The Romans leveled this Temple in 70 AD, just as Jesus had predicted a generation earlier. "Not one stone will be left on another," he had said.

The first generation of Christians won hearts and minds by sacrificing for others, even at the cost of their lives. They met in homes or handy public areas or in the tunnels under the city of Rome. And they flourished.

But as time went on the Roman rulers decided to stop killing Christians and to work with them, since the Christians had such an impact with their caring for the down and out people everywhere they went. Burning them as torches in garden parties or throwing them to the lions and gladiators only made Jesus' teachings more powerful.

Once in a privileged position in society, the Christians began to build their own temples to worship in. Soon there were cathedrals, such as St. Sophia in what is now Istanbul and many in Europe. Clergy became an elite ruling class instead of the servants of all as Jesus had instructed. As Europe crumbled toward anarchy and the Roman world weakened, the church filled the gap. The result was the reverse of what Jesus wanted. The Crusades are one of the egregious examples of things going in the wrong direction.

In our time this confusion is still marring the message of the Prince of Peace. While we have Mother Teresa and others who serve in the style of Jesus, pouring out their lives for others, not themselves, we also have profiteers hustling for profits by marketing the health and wealth gospel you often find on TV. (Not all TV religion is corrupt. But much of it is questionable.)

I have seen this even in Africa and Latin America, where the message of the person who said he didn't even own a place to lay his head at night has been turned into a scheme to get God to give you what you want in this world.

Jesus would be rolling over in his grave—if that were where he is.

But Jesus predicted even this. He said that as the end draws near there would be few true followers. The love of most would grow cold. Imposters would abound. Read the Gospel of Matthew, chapter 24.

Thankfully, many followers of Jesus are repenting of this corruption of his message and spending themselves unstintingly for others—both in their use of time and their money.

Jesus insists that his true followers live for the unseen kingdom that is the true reality, rather than for the things of this world that will pass away. Digging deeper into what this world offers is not the way to go. Reaching higher into God's world is the way to real life.

They say you can't take it with you. But Jesus says he can take you with him.

Embracing Suffering

As a follower of Jesus, I have deliberately embraced a life of suffering. One cannot follow Jesus and do otherwise. This is not easy. It is not popular. Many who teach Christianity ignore this call to suffering and thus misrepresent Christ.

The way of the worldly wise is to reject suffering—or at least to try to escape from it as quickly as possible.

Suffering is a stumbling block for those who think that religion and especially Christianity is designed to escape suffering. People eagerly listen to preachers of religion who promise a path to health and prosperity in this world. This is a false gospel.

So why consider the Gospel of Jesus at all? If the Gospel is what it claims—good news—why this embrace of suffering?

Suffering embraced is paradoxical. One is not surprised at this.

Jesus turned almost everything on its head—to give is to gain, to lose is to win, to die is to live.

Proposition One: The follower of Jesus embraces a life of suffering but never a life of disappointment.

Proposition Two: The follower of the world flees a life of suffering but experiences a life of disappointment.

Some clarifications.

By embracing suffering I do not mean seeking pain. It is natural to avoid pain and suffering when possible. No masochism here. Pain and suffering come to us constantly. Some of it is mild, some excruciating. Some of it is fleeting, some chronic. We have no control over this in many cases. We try to avoid or lessen suffering whenever we can. At some time, however, pain is going to claim us. Sometimes the suffering will be extreme.

To embrace suffering is to accept the fact that suffering in one degree or another is inescapable. At that point, I am wise to embrace it. Not merely endure it. But embrace it.

The first followers of Jesus—those who knew him personally or at most second hand—absorbed this astounding call to suffering. They had seen Jesus actually do it. And they followed him down that path. Several generations of Christians followed the apostles' example of suffering and even martyrdom.

Jesus purposely embraced the ultimate suffering as he walked unflinching to execution—engineered by the Jewish religious authorities and carried out by the pragmatic Roman occupiers at Pilate's craven command.

Jesus' choice did not bring disappointment—quite the opposite. It resulted in glory beyond imagining.

Why is the cross the symbol of Jesus' kingdom? Because it is the path to his exaltation to the highest place in both heaven and earth. Because he endured the infinite suffering of the cross he is now exalted to the infinite glory above all kingdoms and powers whether in heaven or on earth—the universe of space and time and realms beyond space and time.

Suffering in and of itself is evil and one never seeks it for its own sake.

What, then, motivated Jesus to embrace torture and death when all alternatives faded? It was the prospect of joy. Jesus, the author and finisher of the faith, embraced suffering because of the joy that would result from it. Read Hebrews 12:2.

This sets Jesus apart. He walked into suffering with his eyes wide open. He probably could have avoided it if he had chosen to forsake his principles. But he embraced it and was not disappointed.

This is what a follower of Jesus signs on for. The disciple is not above his master, Jesus said. If I have suffered, so you will suffer. To follow me is not to gain health and prosperity in this world. The world will hate you and inflict pain upon you just for following in my footsteps. But rejoice! The reward is unbelievably great!

This is why I too embrace suffering when it comes my way. Suffering hurts. I do not enjoy it. But this experience does not defeat me. It does not disappoint me. In Jesus I see the final outcome—a joy that enables me to seek for strength to endure instead of looking for a quick exit.

A secular person, by contrast, is always looking for any means of avoiding suffering. Since some suffering is unavoidable, disappointment sets in. Even anger. There are some exceptions to this. But it holds as a general truth—an insight into the mindset of people, especially those in privileged circumstances who try to surround themselves with the comfort and security that money provides.

What is the final outcome for those who shrink from suffering? The result is a shriveling of the soul and the loss of the approval of the only one who matters in the end—God. "They have their reward," said Jesus. But it is a shrunken reward that evaporates with one's final breath.

What kind of suffering are we talking about?

The obvious kinds of suffering need no elaboration. Trauma. Illness. Injury. Rejection, persecution, poverty, isolation are among the severe sufferings of mankind.

But there are also subtle sufferings. Realizing that our everyday experience is often flat or meaningless is a kind of suffering. The realization that life wears us down slowly, like the slow erosion of the mountains or the slow sloughing off of tire treads over 60,000 miles of highway driving. The minor betrayals, the small bruises that deflate our happiness. Even a life filled with mostly positive experiences can, in my case at least, leave a film of unfulfillment, subtle though it may be.

Eastern religions highlight this feeling. Life is suffering. Escape is desirable. By much striving over many lifetimes one may hope for *moksha*, release from all individual consciousness.

The western way is to ignore the underlying disillusionment of life by personal pleasure and affluence—let the good times roll. Keep busy so you don't think about it.

Suffering can refine the soul; draw us close to Jesus and to others; give us a heart of compassion. I will embrace suffering as Jesus did.

As a follower of Jesus, in the midst of pain and even tragedy, the deep bass notes of joy can be felt, promising the eventual explosion of the full orchestra as the Hallelujah Chorus fills the heavens and thrills the souls of all who, as Jesus, embraced the suffering that came to them in life for the sake of the joy that is the reward of those who follow in his footsteps.

Heart for Africa

Janine Maxwell is a remarkable woman of faith. A successful businesswoman, her advertising company had accounts with Campbell Soup, Kellogg, and other large corporations.

And then she went to Africa to help out with a project aiding widows and children who were victims of the HIV-AIDS epidemic.

Devastated by their plight, she could not rest. The words of Jesus, found in the Gospel of Matthew, kept coming to her mind. Jesus had said this to his followers as he commissioned them to go into the world to serve God.

"For when I was hungry you did not feed me; when thirsty, you gave me nothing to drink. When a stranger you did not shelter me. I needed clothes but you never clothed me. When sick or in prison you never visited." Then they will say, "Lord when did we ever see you hungry or thirsty, a stranger, or needing clothes, or sick or imprisoned and did not help?" He will reply, "I mean this—when you did not do for the nobodies in society, you failed to do it for me."

Janine went home, quit her business career and started a non-profit called Heart for Africa (not the same as Heart of Africa if you should try to Google her website).

She reported to a small group of us meeting at West Congregational Church in Haverhill, MA, this weekend for world outreach emphasis week. She told us that they now had a large tract of land in Swaziland, which is remarkable since the king owns 70% of the land area of Swaziland. A business friend purchased this land for them to build orphanages and to farm. It is high in the hills and has springs to supply abundant water.

As they went to explore the hilltop they found a huge eucalyptus grove and about 500 children squatting there. These AIDS orphans had dug burrows at the roots of the trees and were living there under makeshift shelters. Their food consisted of leaves and bark of the trees! No adults anywhere.

In other locations kids whose parents had died were living in the family shack alone trying to scrounge enough to live on. In one house there were several children being cared for by the oldest boy, aged 12.

Janine now travels to Africa several times a year with teams of volunteers to build houses and plant gardens for widows willing to take on up to ten orphans. They raise money so the children can have school uniforms and pay the school fees that many African nations require of each student.

Simple things are difficult there. The women will walk miles to carry water for the seedlings they plant when they could use household grey water from cooking and washing. The government does little or nothing to assist the poor. Aid sent to these countries from generous governments such as the USA and Canada and Europe is black-marketed, seldom reaching the people who need it. Doctors from the USA take vacation time to hold free clinics and dispense medicines.

If present trends continue Swaziland could collapse as most of the population dies or is too sick to work. Unemployment is currently 70%

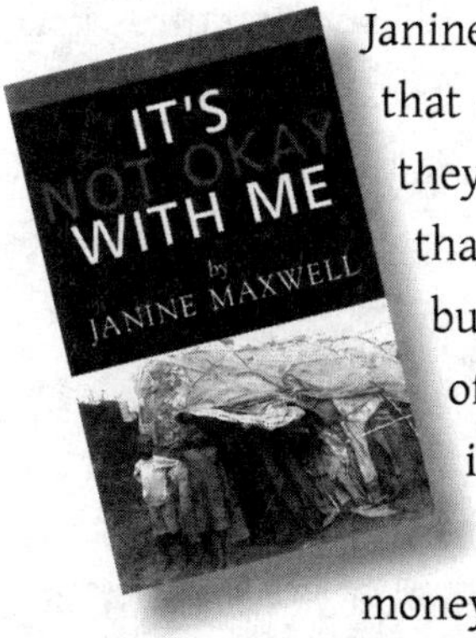

Janine wrote her story—*It's Not OK with Me*—that calls upon individuals to decide what they are to do about this. Janine sensed that God was calling her to cash in her business career and become a champion of the poor. She asked us to consider if God is calling us to pray or to knit warm caps for the children or to give money for blankets or to join a group going to Africa for three weeks next summer to help in the effort.

She did not lay a guilt trip on us. It's up to each person to decide to what extent and how we are to be our brother's keeper. There are needs right here where we live as well as across the oceans.

Just pray this prayer, she said. "Lord, what would You have me to do?"

Janine is not likely to make the news or be featured in our big magazines. That's too bad, for there are thousands of ordinary people like her who roll up their sleeves and do something while so many just talk or look the other way.

It was inspiring to meet her.

88 Coincidence or God?

"There *Is* a Mind Behind It." Is the Bible an expression of the mind of God? Is a Creative Mind behind the universe?

My thesis is this: to answer "no" to either question requires an act of faith far greater than the faith of religion, more particularly, monotheistic religion. It is more credible to see here evidence for God.

The empirical data I appeal to are the following.

First, Psalm 22. Here are the lyrics sung to a popular tune of the day by King David. David would likely have been in the Top Ten if there had been such a register for the great singers of 10th century B.C.

Second, Genesis chapter 1 where the creation account is given as a prologue to the revelation Hebrew people believed came from God, the mighty creator of the space-time universe.

Let's start with the Psalm.

King David wrote Psalm 22 long before he became king. He and his rag-tag band of brothers were on the run for years, hounded by a bloodthirsty, possibly mad, definitely jealous King Saul, who was hunting him down in the Judean desert, southeast of Jerusalem.

As in all great poetry, David conjures up striking imagery to vent the anguish of his soul. God is far away and ignores David's cries for help. God helped the Israelites in the past when they were in distress—but not me, he laments. I must be a worm. Everyone insults and mocks me as a god-forsaken failure.

This is incomprehensible, since David has known the love of God since childhood.

Bulls and lions circle around as his strength ebbs, his tongue sticks to the roof of his mouth as he eats the dust of death. Dogs lick their chops and evil enemies stab his hands and feet. He can see his bones sticking out of his wasted body as his enemies strip off his clothes and gamble to see who gets what.

Here the song takes a turn from gloom and doom to hope and assurance.

David speaks of a day when he will praise God in the worship assembly of the people. God has finally heard and rescued him.

As a devout Jew, Jesus, living a thousand years later than David, memorized this Psalm along with may other passages of the Hebrew Scriptures. As he spoke them during his crucifixion a series of astounding parallels emerge.

Let's summarize key phrases.

My God, my God, why have you forsaken me? I cry out but you do not answer. Verses 1 and 2

I am scorned by men and despised by the people. All who see me mock me..., [saying] "he trusts in the Lord, let the Lord rescue him; let God deliver since he delights in him." Verses 6-8

I am poured out as water and my bones are out of joint; my heart is like wax; it has melted away within me. My strength has evaporated...and my tongue sticks to the roof of my mouth.... A crowd of evil men encircles me, piercing my hands and feet. I can count every one of my bones; people gape at me and gloat. Dividing up my garments, they throw dice for my clothes. Verses 14-18

You who fear the Lord, praise him! For he has not despised the suffering of this afflicted one.... All the far reaches of the earth will remember and turn to him, for the LORD is sovereign over all nations. Verses 23-28

Add to this another phrase from David's lyrics in Psalm 34:20, where David is rejoicing for his escape from the clutches of a neighboring king. God "protects all his bones, not one of them will be broken."

Now notice how Jesus quotes from this Psalm as he hangs on the cross, "My God. My God, why have you forsaken me?" Matthew 27:46 and Mark 15:34

This phrase taken alone is easy to explain without appealing to God, since many rabbis of Jesus' times likely recited this in times of suffering. But here comes the remarkable part.

The crowd of onlookers hurls insults at Jesus while soldiers gamble for his clothes. How can one attribute that detail of the Psalm to chance? The detail about water pouring out precisely fits the spear thrust of a soldier that penetrated Jesus' pericardium, releasing blood and water. This showed that Jesus was already dead so that his bones (unlike the legs of the other two criminals along side him) would not need to be smashed—not one of his bones was broken. In crucifixion bones are wracked out joint, dehydration parches the tongue, and hands and feet are pierced. The details here are precise and numerous, eliminating coincidence as a believable explanation of how the Psalm and the Gospel accounts mesh.

To top it off, the Psalm indicates that this is not the end of the story. This person who suffered so horribly will be remembered by his God and cause people from many nations to praise the Lord.

To explain this parallel away as some rare stroke of literary luck rather than as a revelation from God requires more faith than to admit its divine inspiration.

I claim that an examination of the creation account in the poetry of Genesis chapter one also leads one to the same conclusion. I intend to argue this in a further post.

Foundations for Following Jesus

BASIC FOUNDATIONS FOR ANY FOLLOWER OF JESUS OF NAZARETH

Purpose

My hope is to present the basic teachings of Jesus, addressed to any person who wants to know whether or not to follow him.

Goal

My goal is to clear away the confusion—let's call it misrepresentation—about who Jesus is and what he taught. Much of this confusion has come from the organized religion of Christianity. While I know I must be a part of this body of believers (Jesus requires it), nevertheless I must test what various churches teach and their practices by the Gospel itself. While this cannot here be done in detail we will look at the basics. It is not that hard, since the writings about Jesus and his original followers, while profound, are not lengthy.

The Irreducible Foundation

Jesus reverses much of our common sense "default" thinking about God and what God expects of us. We must grasp this clearly. I cannot emphasize this enough. This is the place where most of us can easily go wrong and end up thinking the exact opposite of what a follower of Jesus should embrace. So here are the essentials.

A. God is God. I am not God. God knows what is best; I do not. God alone can run the universe and bring about the highest fulfillment of his plan in the end. I cannot do this and cannot give God any of my own wisdom because my thoughts are mostly foolishness by comparison.

B. God is not my servant. I must be willing to be his servant.

C. Jesus requires that I completely give all of myself—my hopes and dreams, my plans, my time, my stuff—to God. This does not mean keeping some things for my own control. It means giving everything I am and everything I have to him. Everything. This radical requirement is where most people, even Christians, go wrong. We want to give God this and that, but not everything. But all or nothing is the only deal Jesus offers.

Let's apply this to life.

1. Prayer

For most people in any religion prayer is a way to get what you want from the Higher Power. Jesus does not teach this. Jesus did not practice this. If we want to follow Jesus, what must we do? We must turn over everything to God. "Your kingdom come, your will be done on earth as it is in heaven." This phrase in the Lord's Prayer is key. Jesus went on to detail what this means. Leave everything and follow Jesus. Everything. (Try to ponder for a minute what everything means in your case.) The people Jesus accepted as his core followers left everything to follow him. While many of the hundreds who followed him during his lifetime and the many thousands that followed him in the first century continued to live in their communities, they gave all their previous hopes, dreams, and stuff to Jesus. And their prayers were not prayers asking God for what they wanted. Their prayers were always for what would promote the Gospel.

While many of them prayed to be protected from suffering and death, they prayed as Jesus did when he was facing death—not my will be done, but thy will be done, O God my Father.

Prayer is not asking God for things we want or think we need, as most of us assume. Prayer is aligning myself with God's program, with God's passion, asking for what God wants and nothing more. Most Christians do not grasp this. That is why they get discouraged. "I asked God for health, for help, for what I needed, and God did not come through for me." This causes many people to give up following Jesus. "It doesn't work for me," they say. Notice the assumption here—God exists to give me what I want—at least the good things I want. Jesus never taught this. Nor did he live this way. He declares that if we choose to follow him we too will often live a life of hardship, even persecution, perhaps death. It's about God and the kingdom, not about me and my plan for my life.

2. Lifestyle

We often think of ourselves with our hands stretched

out each day so God can fill our hands with his blessings. But Jesus did not live this way. If we follow him we will not live this way.

Instead, our hands will be stretched out to others all the time so they can take from our hands what we have to offer them, even if it means we go without. This is how Jesus lived. As a follower, this is how I should live.

We are tempted to get up each morning and run over our day's activities in our minds and then ask God to give us what we need to get it all accomplished.

What we should do is to ask God to prompt us to see opportunities to bless others all through the day. Talking with people along the way. Doing our work, getting our shopping done, interacting with our family members, our default attitude should be this—how can I give to this person? Maybe it's only a smile or a word of thanks. Maybe it's a helping hand or some of my stuff. Above all it's a word about God that can get them to think about the key thing in life—where we stand in relation to him.

Jesus constantly focused on the needs of the people around him and he ministered to them. It was about them, not about himself. This is my model. I am a giver not a taker. I seek to bless others more than to be blessed. Although Jesus taught that by living this life of giving, we would actually receive the deep satisfaction that comes from serving God. It is in giving that we receive.

Proclaiming Good News

SATURDAY, OCTOBER 28, 2006

"It was a dark and stormy night...."

Actually, it's a dark and stormy day in Haverhill, MA as I pack for India. This storm was born in the turbulent Pacific last week to El Nina, who with her consort El Nino attacks North America repeatedly. Now, over New England, a triple convergence assails us with winds approaching hurricane force, together with pelting rain.

But I sit comfortably near the woodstove, hoping that Ellie will be OK as I board Continental Sunday afternoon to head for India. I have called our oil burner guy - Cliff Peters, an old tenant of ours when we owned 105 Bellevue Avenue (where Rachel and Dale spent a stressful year early in their marriage) to resurrect our aged oil burner before the frosts get severe. Cousin Harry Carlson sold me that old Federal-Huber furnace when we built this house in 1970. So we have no basis for complaints!

Friend Jim Herrick has become my personal chauffeur to Logan and back on my recent trips to India and Kenya - bless his heart. So at 2 p.m. he will load my bags and deliver me to the terminal. This year I am flying to Newark, whence I can get a non-stop to Delhi. This seemed like a good idea last August when that plot to blow up planes to the USA was thwarted. *Maybe 11 hours in one plane, flying over Greenland, Finland and Russia isn't a bad idea!*

So I'll put on my elastic socks to keep blood from settling in my aging legs. I'll also get up and walk the cabin aisles frequently. I'm even bringing along my new stretch-cord exercise kit, determined as I am to avoid getting out of shape during the cold months. (It now takes me too long to get back in shape in the spring, as the chain saw and wood-splitting chores inflict me with increasing muscle pain. I'm not wild about pain any more.) So I ask your prayers for my journey.

I get into Delhi on Monday evening (although it's ten hours ahead of EST, so it will be Monday morning here) and am taken by Saju Varghese to the Delhi guest room. By 6 a.m. he will see that I am on the train to Dehra Dun. It's a 5-hour trip through the lush plains dotted with rice paddies and then into the hillier terrain near Dehra Dun. There faculty brothers from New Theological College will pick me up. By car we travel another several miles to the campus, dodging the ubiquitous cows that wander *everywhere* in India.

Ensconced in the lovely Guest House, I'll take a sleeping aid and zonk out for 10 hours. Rengit (REN-jeet, the cook) will wake me in time for breakfast before morning chapel. He is not a Christian (yet) but has become a friend to all who visit the campus. And that would include you, should you wish to come to visit India.

Just a word about cows before I sign off.

Hindu lore says that when a mother stops nursing her boy or girl around age 3, the milk of the cow sustains her children. The basis of all *puja* (sacrifices) is *ghee* - what we call butter, more or less. One sees milk in tiny bowls under trees where Hindus make their offerings. So the cow is divine, the source of all sustenance for life. When a motorist killed a cow a few years back a mob lynched and killed the driver. Officials pressed no charges. One of the gurus said that the life of one cow is worth more than the life of many humans.

This is the context in North India, formerly Hindustan. Pray that I may add a spiritual value to the training of men and women whom God is calling to proclaim goods news in this wonderful nation teeming with people who have never heard the Gospel.

Blow Me Down

TUESDAY, OCTOBER 31, 2006

Well -blow me down! – as Popeye used to say.

With a driver not showing up on Sunday at 2 pm to chauffeur me to Logan, things got off on a shaky note. Tim Chechowitz was the third frantic call I made and he drove my car home from the airport. Even with the delay I was there about the time I had planned on. Sunday traffic is great! And no ceilings fell on us as we sailed through the new tunnel in Boston. Big Dig became Big Bust. Scary.

But the nice lady helped me do my first touch-screen check-in. Sorta like Wal-Mart or Home Depot self-checkout only different. Through with screening—they only took my water bottle this time – I am a slow learner on these ever-changing regulations. *Blow me down!*

Flying in the Big Blow (50+ mile winds) made for a few bumps en route to Newark, but we landed safely enough even though a couple of runways were shut down due to high winds. 49-minute flight time. But Newark – is HUGE now. Three terminals with about 40 gates each. A neat air train takes me on a monorail to terminal C. Trains appear every 3 minutes and whisk you around a big loop.

But here an embarrassing episode intrudes. (I strongly suggest you skip to the next paragraph right now.) You see, showering just before I left Haverhill and giving my last hugs to Ellie, I found I had packed all my underwear in the BIG suitcase, which was downstairs. So after the shower I rummaged through my dresser to see if anything showed up. Aha! Yes – a pair of bikini briefs that I hadn't worn since I last felt like a teenager, were tempting me from the back of the drawer. "OK," says I ,"I can do that!" I'm feeling like old times now. Until they began to let me down. (I told you to skip this paragraph! It's probably too late now, right?) Standing there waiting for the air train I notice the garment is kept from puddling about my feet only by the fact that I am wearing slacks. So I am discreetly trying to reach into pocket A to sneak it up a notch. Then pocket B and so on around the compass points on my pants. Try that three or four times with little success and you wished you had opened the big suitcase while you were still in the privacy of your own home! After waddling around the next terminal to find a men's room, I find a way to put myself properly together. Now I know why old men don't wear those things if they have any sense....

13 hours on a Boeing 777 is along time. And when they stack you up over Delhi for a while waiting for runways to clear, you know how far it is from NJ to Delhi: 7788 miles, more or less.

Then it hits you. What you forgot – because you wanted to forget – about India. Smoke. Smog. Smell. India is said to have the world's cleanest people in the world's dirtiest environment. Yep

– still there – families sleeping on blankets in the terminals and sidewalks—homeless.

It's 11 pm. Light traffic here is heavy traffic in Boston. You drive with your horn. In fact buses and lorries (that's a big truck to you, McKenzie and Walker) have signs painted on the back—"Horn Please." It reminds me of geese in flight, each one honking away just to let the others know you're coming up on the inside of the ever-changing flight pattern. Red lights? Simply means you look both ways to see if you can scoot through on breaks between cross traffic cars. Need to get ahead of the 3-wheel jitney spewing smoke at you? Just go down the wrong side of the traffic island for a block then squeeze back onto your side (left side) of the road.

Here's a scene not seen every day—a parade of white Brahmin cattle, some hitched to rickety carts—along the curb side—some 50-60 of them. Cows have no lights. Neither do some of the cars and scooters beeping their way through the traffic. People walking on the streets; dodging vehicles of all types while crossing four to six lanes. Dogs. Old and young. Two or three people on one scooter. It's wild! Yet no one seems to get into trouble. I could really enjoy it driving here. *Those rules don't apply to me.... They're just suggestions.*

Up at 5 a.m. to catch the train for Dehra Dun. Peaceful, those trains.... I got to finish and make notes on a library book: *Islam for Western Minds* by Henry Drummond. I'll tell you about it—but not now. It's time to rest a bit in the quiet Guest House at New Theological College. I have my first class tonight.

You could *blow me down* with a feather.

Slap Me Down and Pick Me Up

I don't know which to share first. Since I am not known for humility (except among those whom I can fool, not my family, for sure) I will do the upbeat first and then the downbeat.

Pick Me Up!

For whatever cause, when I come to a place like New Theological College here in north India, I feel a pickup. A cynic would say, "Sure – anybody would. You get your room cleaned, your meals to order by a chef, and people who copy your syllabus and deliver it to your classroom, others who prepare tea twice a day (one good legacy left by the British Raj), with no telephone to bug you. You get to go to a clean desk and use a computer with tech people ready to troubleshoot for you, and people who smile every time you look at them."

But that's not it, really.

Did you see the old movie about missionary Eric Liddell called *Chariots of Fire*? He was an Olympic champion runner from England—the one who would not compete on Sunday because it was the Lord's Day. (I really wish I had that kind of courage. But I don't. I know I would have found some way to rationalize to save embarrassment. I have the philosopher's gift: find a plausible reason for anything!) Eric was conflicted about his commitment to running and his call to serve the Lord. Explaining to his sister his passion for track he said this memorable line: "*When I run I feel the pleasure of God.*"

When I am in a place like this using my gifts in a small but not insignificant way I too feel the pleasure of God. There is a deep satisfaction there. It's beyond happiness. It's a kind of spiritual joy hard to describe. As I walked to the Guest House under the moon the other night, this moment of elevation picked me up. I knew, despite all the expense and hassle of flying half way around the world, that this was where I was supposed to be. Making a difference, no matter how small, is such a satisfaction. I was telling my students yesterday that on those days when I want to get away from everything and do something just for me—to pamper myself a bit (they tell me I deserve it)—I usually feel pretty good. *But not great.* But at the end of a day where I went out of the way to make a difference for good in someone's life—be it doing a chore or taking someone to the store or fixing a loose bolt—I feel great. That's why we were put on earth—to help each other in times of joy and in times of sorrow.

So that's the *"Pick Me Up!"*

Now for the "Slap Me Down."

I look at the students here and I am chastised. I listen to their stories. Many have little help when they are ill—medicines are too expensive, even here in India where everything is half price to me. Fees are always a challenge. Some face rejection by their families. Yet they work at their tools for ministry. They yield to God's call to a life that for many is one of hardship with risk of bodily harm, even death. They know what it is to walk by faith. This cuts my soul.

I have so much more than they. I have more stuff. I have opportunities that my education and my wealth afford me. I can shield myself, protect myself. I can play it safe. I hardly know what sacrifice means when I look at these followers of Jesus, let alone at Jesus himself. These students rise at 5 a.m. for a voluntary prayer service of their own making. They gather after supper at 7 p.m. and ask for Dave Walker or some other visiting minister to talk to them about Christ and the Gospel. The limit of my devotion is to pray for a while in shadows of the dawn from the warmth of my bed.

I know that asceticism and fanaticism are over the top. I learned that studying church history. But I'm coming clean. I do not know much about following God with true passion. It's in my head—I truly do grasp it. I can teach it and preach it. But true religion is emptying myself and my treasure now in the real world.

So I am "slapped down." It's something I need to pay attention to. I know I am thought to be a generous, caring, and giving person. But that's in the eyes of men. Before God I have along way to go. And I need to go on my knees. I fear that American followers of the Way (such as myself) know next to nothing about walking the talk. We give a lot. But there is small sacrifice in it.

I always tell my students that there are no U-Hauls on hearses. But am I really living in the light of this old Gospel-song truth: *This world is not my home, I'm just a-passing through, and I cain't feel at home in this world anymore?*

Will Somebody help me? There's nothing wrong with enjoying life—sure thing. But is the danger to my soul that I will not spend enough time enjoying the good life? Yeah, right!

Slap me down: then you can pick me up.

He Promised Never to Leave Me

NOVEMBER 3, 2006

After a breakfast of porridge, toast and chai, I was introduced to Adrienne Thompson and her aid, Caroline, of the Parker Foundation in Richmond, VA. This family foundation funds projects for Christian ministry, mostly international. The young (25-ish) women do the traveling for the foundation to scope out worthy projects. New Theological College here has been awarded some funds and they have come to interview deans and faculty on behalf of the home office. Possibly you will see an article in *Christianity Today* this season including their findings, entitled: *What It Means to Be a Counter-cultural Christian in Today's World.* Each culture (including the USA) needs voices to speak truth for God to the power structures of government and education. The women are staying here for one day before heading off to Hyderabad and other India locations to gather information.

In the Chapel sermon, a senior student chose the text I Peter 1:1-9, explaining how our trials refine us to reflect the glory of God in our lives. I thought of our dear friends Barry Noonan and Patrick and Katie, in the loss of wife/mother Maryann this week to cancer. What sorrow must be theirs as they undergo this trial.

While we prayed for her healing more than once, she has now experienced the final healing that God effects when He calls us to himself. But broken hearts result, often crying out, "Why? Why now?" The hymn this morning was an old one, set to Indian rhythms: *He Promised Never to Leave Me Alone*. This is a hope to comfort and sustain us in sore trials.

I find it illuminating to be in another context like this away from home. There I can fool myself that the world is a safe place to call home. But this world is often at war with goodness and justice and shalom. Here I am face to face with poverty of goods and of spirit, for the battle of good and evil is more obvious. Reports come daily from graduates who are deep in the danger of battle as they bring good news to people not always welcoming. We hear of persecutions and threats. We know that the worldwide community of faith is, as always, under siege.

And yet there is joy and thankfulness everywhere evident. I am always learning from brothers and sisters here.

Yesterday at my evening session, Dr. M.T. Cherian agreed to lecture on Hindu ethics. Masterfully he had the students interacting and laughing while he drove home the concepts of karma and dharma: *find your assigned place in life (according to caste) and do your duty without fail for god and god alone, not your own desires. Then you may rise in the next re-birth and eventually achieve moksha—liberation. Your life now is exactly what you have created by your past, reaping what you have sown.* A brilliant example of good pedagogy.

And to top off my amazement, my house mate, Dave Walker, shared some of his experiences over breakfast with the women visiting for the day. He is a former pastor who has gone into mission work on his own. Traveling to places all over the world, he preaches mostly to the common people, wins converts, starts churches, trains leaders in a few small Bible schools he sets up. What he has accomplished is astounding. One man making a difference—sort of like St. Paul. He is away from home about 36 weeks a year with his wife's encouragement. (Sounds suspicious to me. Yet he says they have a great marriage, having raised 5 boys now adults. He now has the first girl in the line for several generations – a granddaughter in Detroit now 5 months old.)

When speaking in a public hall in a city near Calcutta the police came in to arrest him, since it is against India law for foreigners to proselytize. He stood up to the officer, who was drunk, and the Lord gave him the right words so he was not charged. A church started there and is going to this day.

Another time he was in prison for 9 months in India. In yet another location he was brought to the police station where the charge man took his passport and visa and was adamant about prosecuting him. But almost miraculously the man had a sudden change of heart and said, "It's OK, you can preach here. But I am assigning an officer to protect you because there is a mob growing that wants to kill you!"

Another time in Nigeria he got word of some who wanted to harm him. The brothers, not having a basket or a wall to lower him over (see Acts 9:23-25), smuggled him to safety. Dave now has work ongoing in Malawi, Rwanda, Brazil, India, Nigeria and I forget where else.

Dave is so self-deprecating and humble. I had no idea for four days that I was sleeping every night next to a giant for God.

Dave told me that when he was pastoring, missionaries coming to his church would say we appreciate your funds but we really ask your prayers. "Oh sure," he would think, "that's good PR." But when he got out on the battlefield he realized that while funds are a blessing, the prayers are a matter of life and death.

So it is that each of us, stumbling as we do, add a little to the kingdom work as we strive to be faithful to the small tasks assigned to us. I am a little more humble than when I left Haverhill last week. As the old hymn puts it: *"He promised never to leave me, never to leave me alone."*

You can take that two ways. Both apply to me today.

A Greater Light

FRIDAY, NOVEMBER 10, 2006

On this campus in Uttaranchal, north India, the walkway lights go off at 4:45. It is still night and except for the beams from the moon this morning I would have needed my flashlight (one of those "shake and shine" types I sent for on TV) to get down the steps on the paths that circle the campus.

At 5 the bells ring to wake the girls in the women's hostel nestled safely between the guesthouse and the faculty apartments. The college is supremely *in loco parentis* here. I slip quietly by to breathe the cool air—probably 62 degrees I would guess. Students keep asking "are you not cold?" My shadow is sharp since the moon is waning but gibbous, several hours from setting. First light timidly approaches the mountains to the east.

By the time I am making my fifth round dawn is beginning to paint the pastel watercolors that will deepen over the eastern horizon. I notice my shadow is losing strength. When sunrise comes, even if the disc is hidden behind the mountains for a while, the shadow will fade and disappear.

Another sun arises. "Arise, shine, for thy light has come; and the glory of the Lord shines upon thee." Drawing near in heart to the "Light that has come into the world" the shadows weaken and die. Just as I can see that the moon is still there when I search the sky for it, it no longer casts a shadow. So the greater light of the sun of righteousness dispels all darkness and shadows of the night.

Today I will walk in the light as He is in the light. I will have fellowship with brothers and sisters here and around the world. I will reflect His light by God's grace in all I do. I am no longer a child of the shadows, for the sun of righteousness has arisen with healing for me in his wings. I face today with joy and confidence.

Now that the sun has ascended beyond the peaks of the mountains I notice that the quad has billowing tent pavilions, erected during the night. Is a medieval festival coming? Will I see horsemen with lance and armor competing for the fair ones? Soon I see a banner welcoming children in the name of World Vision.

After chapel I will give my seniors their final exam. A senior destined for tent revival ministry is the preacher. And yes, he is going overtime, etc. to Hosea chapter one. At the end of the service Dr. Samuel, Principal, calls me to the platform to thank me for my service with a brightly packaged small (thankfully) gift. I express thanks for the blessings given by this vibrant community of faith, leaving them with a verse from James chapter seven, verse one: "Trials and tests come in the morning, but joy comes at noon." Everyone laughs except my poor ethics students!

Fast forward> > >

Exams are over. I am snapping photos of the festivities. "Uncle, uncle!" the children cry. I take a picture of some boys near the playground. Then of some girls sitting on the grass having a boxed "Happy Meal." Soon a jumping swarm of giggles clamors for foto, foto. That's the trouble with these digitals—they know they can see themselves a few seconds after the click.

Now music is sounding. On the banked wall the chapel praise team is tuning up. I get a snap of the students singing a gesture song with about 200 kids. Most classes have been cancelled for the day—save for my accursed final exam.

Later a young married couple comes to the guesthouse. He is now teaching here, while his wife is one of the assistants to the Registrar. I had been to their house in a nearby village with Dr. Tim Tennent of Gordon-Conwell Theological Seminary and one-time interim preaching pastor at our church in Haverhill. They have a six-month baby boy. I find it strange that he is unnamed as yet. (I doubt it's like Kenya, where a child is named after a father figure in hopes of sponsorship for school fees, etc. That has happened to me and to my sister Lois who was a missionary teacher there for 11 years.)

They have come for prayer.

What do you want Jesus to do for you today?

I have severe back pain from childbirth. And an occasional pain that goes from my chest to my back shoulder. I want for you to pray for me.

Do you want me to anoint you according to James 5?

So I explain that there is no oil. OK, you can use a few molecules of butter from the kitchen. So I pray according to God's will that Jesus will heal her.

Her husband also praises God for deliverance from a darkness that deepened in his life since his father's death last spring (detailed in a previous Blog) and asks for a sponsor so he can go for his higher degree in two years when the college can release him. He is so humble, so gifted, so worthy. I will pray his needs will be met at the right time.

As they go I give them some snacks I don't need for their kids. And encourage her to find a doctor to find out her shoulder problem. Someone told her it might need a muscle relaxant. And she said she had had a spinal shot for the birth. I tell her how agonizing the aftermath was for my wife when the doctor used a spinal block when our Rachel came into the world.

We part, our faces glowing with the joy of our God.

The greater light! The greater light!

Mr. Toad's Wild Ride

The most gasp-filled hour in road race history might be the hour-long ride to Indira Gandhi International Airport in Delhi. A thousand near misses leaves me exhausted. It is dusk going on night. Highway lights are dim in many places. Some cars and trucks have one or no headlights. And the air is full of dust and smoke. So it was really hard to see the elephant, mahout atop, plodding down a thoroughfare in Delhi! Amazingly, I have never seen cars stopped due to an accident or even a bump or scrape, nor a dead dog, pig, or cow along the road, much less an elephant. (And we think hitting a moose is dangerous—think of hitting an elephant...!)

At the terminal four score taxis and cars are stopping for disembarkation of passengers while others jockey to extricate themselves from the tangle—like a worm trying to get out of a box of night crawlers.

The queue starts on the sidewalk. In ten minutes I am inside the terminal with my carryon and a big bag that is not nearly so heavy now that I have delivered my colleagues' extra textbooks to the librarian at New Theological College.

Immediately I am in a second queue. They screen only your checked bags here, right by the front door, putting a white band around each piece that says "Indian Airlines Security Checked Delhi." OK, one down.

There's no signage in this huge hall. You have to get close enough to read the TV screen each airline has over each of its check in stations. What the heck – I'll go left. Wrong! I ask one of the numberless uniformed people where to find Continental. "Back—go back."

I've never seen so many personnel. Soldiers in khaki, some with bamboo-looking batons, others with really old sub-machine guns. And guys in white shirts rounding up the trolleys, which are free for use here. Of course one thing India has is cheap labor—more sensible than putting motors in everything. Blue uniformed people herding folks to this check-in counter or that. Women in red jackets (Indians like red—it's in their flag) and navy skirts checking us. "Sir, did you pack your bag yourself? Did anyone give you anything to take? Has it been in your possession?" This drill happens to me twice in twenty minutes. "Do you have anything in your carry-on with batteries?" "Oh yes, my camera has four AA." "Anything else?" "Not that I can think of." "No cell phone?" "Oh, yes the cell phone—I haven't used it since I got to India! Sorry." "OK. Sir."

(BTW, at the college in India I am "Sir." At Northern Essex Community College I am "Who?")

At the final screening there is no concern for shoes, unlike the USA (probably due to Richard Reid, the would-be shoe bomber). But I dump everything in my pockets into the plastic bin—it's easier that way. In the queue my turn comes next. I go through the "rose arbor" labeled "Gents" after which one undergoes the wand. Pretty intimate, too. Women go through the ladies' gate and then behind a modesty screen where a madam supposedly gives her the wand once-over. (I mean, how would I know?) This is so different from the high tech whole body "air puff" scanners you stand in at the new Liberty Airport at Newark.

Now I am at the gate. It is after midnight. We are taking off in a Boeing 777 for non-stop 16-hour flight to Newark. I must say goodbye to India. It's been a wild ride!

Speaking of saying goodbye, as I was grading finals in the guesthouse the night before I left, a young man came to the hallway. "You don't remember me, do you?" "Ashish!" I cry, rising to hug this friend I haven't seen for two years. "Don't tell me it's you!"

(BTW—you pronounce his name like a sneeze—or maybe a minced oath, depending on the degree of excitement. My emphasis was definitely the sneeze!)

Ashish is the one I've been telling people about for two years. In 2004 Tim Tennent (Gordon-Conwell Seminary professor, now President of Asbury Theological Seminary), Matthew from a church in Topsfield, and I were looking at a map of India so Asheesh (Gesundheit!) could point out the remote mountain area where God was calling him to start a ministry. It was a place with zero Christians—possibly very dangerous. "What do you need from us as you go?" I had asked him. "I want no money. God will provide for me. But please—your prayers."

So he tells me how God now has blessed the ministry with a school with 64 kids and several teachers. He showed me a video clip on his cell phone of kids reciting the Lord's Prayer two words at a time—that's how they start learning English. All from Hindu families who know the emphasis but want their kids to get ahead and learn English, Also he has three churches already—all by prayer and pluck!

Three years ago I had asked Ashish (Gesundheit!) [Sorry this is starting to sound like a Victor Borge routine] about marriage. He is a very good-looking son-of-a-gun. "I don't think about it," he had said, "Mom will let me know when she's found someone."

Well—BIG NEWS! He is now engaged to Reema, a student I had in my class last year, on December 18. (She got one of the highest scores ever on the national exams!)

"You are coming, Dr. G!"

"I wish I could, but no, I won't be in India then."

"You MUST come to see us wed—and experience a true Indian ceremony."

I truly wished I could go—but it's not exactly a few towns down river from Haverhill.

He (see how cleverly I avoided the Gesundheit by using the pronoun this time?) calls Reema who is across the driveway in the Women's Hostel to have her come to the guesthouse.

They are so devoted—you can see it their eyes. I want a photo. I have to ask them to stand closer to close the 18-inch gap between them for a good picture. They manage to inch a bit closer, but not anywhere near touching. Why? This is India! In the USA a couple 5 weeks from marriage would show no daylight at all between them. I doubt Ashish and Reema have ever kissed. I don't know how they have such discipline in India. But they do—and I admire it.

Well, Mr. Toad, we've had a wild ride together.

When I get to Boston I just might find someone at the airport willing to make this toad a prince!

Big Tests

Some say that life is a test. Will I flunk or pass?

Who grades the test? Maybe the grade is given when people stand by the casket and say truthfully what a fine person I am, or speak polite lies about me that everyone knows is BS.

Or maybe the Heavenly Professor is keeping records of our scores in order to compute a final grade before promoting us or demoting us.

Hindus here in India have a middle view.

There is no one to keep score. But something in the universe makes us reap what we sow—no more, no less. So you keep coming back to re-sit the exam (maybe millions of time) until the equation of my actions comes up with the right answer: zero. "Put in all the pluses and minuses of your good and bad actions, and when it comes out zero, you're done." *Moksha*—release from the suffering at last. At that point, just when a Westerner would be looking forward to the heavenly holidays in a celestial Hawaii now that he's passed life's test and graduated, the Hindu world says I enter an eternal coma. I'm there—but not as me. My drop is lost in the Ocean of the One, whose sound is the relentless "Om."

Here at the college the students are studying for my exam, as from one born out of time. You see, this is the first two weeks of the term. Exams should be far in the future. I am crafting my diabolical questions today! Heh, heh...! No, really – I give the questions ahead of time—they're complex, as one expects in philosophy. No multiple-choice here.

But the preaching class for seniors is taking over morning chapels. And K.J.K. (in India people have no names, just initials) is in the back row with his grading template—sort of like speech class in college. And they speak in English with a colleague translating into Hindi.

Yesterday a young man (who refused to choose a free tie from the collection Dave Walker brought in his traveling thrift shop, since he already had a tie—one—a single tie. Since he can only wear one at a time, let another student take it) in his bright shirt, tie and jacket, called on his buddies to start off with a skit.

A bunch of money-grubbing guys come to the temple to cheat the backwoods bumpkins. Then Jesus and his disciples arrive and drive them out, declaring the temple is a House of Prayer not a den of robbers.

Nice set-up. He goes on with an exposition of the text, closing with an object lesson. Out comes a glass of water from the back of the pulpit. In goes some chemical that makes it look yucky. Then another bromide and it turns wine color as the cleansing power of Jesus' sacrifice starts to work. To my mind, it all broke down there, since he had no chemical to precipitate out the pollutants to make the liquid crystal clear again. I don't know what grade KJK will give him. But it is a nice try—probably an A for ingenuity anyway.

But this morning a girl (oops! I mean young woman) in a canary yellow sari has the service. She is articulate and animated and actually moves the back-benchers. (That's us faculty—who have heard a thousand sermons.) After the benediction, KJK tells me that a few months ago when her turn came to present to the class, she collapsed in tears and couldn't do it. When she enrolled here a couple of years ago, she spoke NO English. On her second try she stumbled through pathetically. On her third try she did OK. And now today—the final exam—one would think English was her mother tongue. What skillful use of vocabulary. What animated gestures. What sincerity of heart. She will be a powerful communicator. And her text and theme was how we should rejoice when we suffer dishonor for Jesus' name, just as the early Christians did and as many former students here are now doing in the hostile environment of north India.

Big tests, for sure.

Life is at the least, a test. Hearts need examination. Motives must be sifted. Plus and minus. Wheat and chaff. Gold and stubble.

I hope my Teacher is as pleased in the end with me as KJK is with this unlikely treasure in Public Speaking 101.

Too Much Time

NOVEMBER 10, 2006

Too Much Time on My Hands

One of the things (dangerous thought it may be) that I enjoy about going on these trips is that my fancy takes flight. My friend, Bill Hopkins, likes to hear my outside-the-box thoughts, but, being a practical man who actually fixes and maintains things that relate to the real world—heavy machinery—says that his job in our friendship is to hold firmly onto my feet. He is fearful that I will rise like a hot-air balloon and wander forever in the clouds.

While I am occupied steadily here with the ethics course and with reading new books and supervising the 6th edition of *The Quest for Truth* (soon to be published here in India), I do have an environment in which new thoughts—or old thoughts revisited—can dance like sugar plums in my head. (A little musical allusion there—*The Nutcracker* by Tchaikovsky, in case you missed it.)

Noting the vitality of the new churches being started by New Theological College graduates here, I see how good it is that they have not yet grown top-heavy. I say *not yet* because it is the nature of energetic enterprises birthed at great sacrifice eventually to become dry structures to maintain. A bureaucracy grows up around it that requires maintenance. And over time we have a sluggish and top-heavy monument trying to preserve, usually unsuccessfully, the vibrancy of previous years.

This certainly has happened thousands of times in the history of the People of the Way of Jesus. And there is nothing wrong with organization and structure. In fact it is essential and valuable. But as someone mentioned about governments, bureaucracies have a way of justifying their own needs until they kill the host upon which they feed. I have observed this—in my own brief lifetime—in the history of congregationalism, where a top-brass elite, ever-further removed from the people, spends resources on things that the people do not want (or would not want if they knew the truth about it) and does not feed the true purpose of the congregations. Fearing now that dark days are coming upon the church—the evangelical church—in our nation, am I wrong in guessing (I am no prophet nor the son of a prophet) that the day of the "successful" church is waning?

Even here in India the news of the latest big name scandal among evangelicals is noised abroad. The damage done by personal sinning among those who should know they "will be judged by a stricter standard" is immeasurable. Bringing shame to our Lord's name is close to unforgivable. So what enables people like this? One (but not the only) cause is that we have forsaken humble holiness for the lure of being power brokers in the world system. We know from two millennia of our history that every one of us needs someone to hold us accountable. The saints of the early church, the medieval church, and the reformed church knew this. The Apostles taught this. The preachers preach it. It is thus inexplicable that the leaders of a congregation do not demand that people who represent the congregation—its public face—submit to accountability. In other words, everyone needs a Bill Hopkins.

Big churches. Big budgets. Big bucks. Big temptations. I wish there were a lay council in every church to probe its pastors and teachers on possible hidden sins. I picture the future as one where smaller congregations—perhaps joining forces for special programs that need critical mass—become the wave of the future. Why do people flock to large churches and megachurches? I suspect that many (not all) go for what is really entertainment value. Better music, preaching, worship space. And perhaps even for anonymity. Do we unconsciously adopt the reigning ethos of our day: *better to look good than be good*? And one result is that pastors get to hide behind their persona so that they insulate themselves from careful soul examination in the presence of "confessors."

Have any of us really done what is costly? Confession (commanded in the New Testament) is one of those costly requirements for those who are walking in the Way. Why is this so rare in our communities of faith today?

Have we ever had to walk by faith in any significant way?

Lord, do what you know it will take to take us deeper! So often we are more hearers of your words than doers.

Trim our church apparatus. Help us to shrink our professional overhead and develop and use the gifts of the laity. Show us more how we can be bi-vocational ministers, just as St. Paul was. The world is on the edge of doom and we are prettying up our suites on Titanic Earth.

"Hey, Bill! Pull me down! The oxygen is thin up here and it's making me a Jeremiah—which I surely do not want!"

Whew—that was close....

Oh! Here's another thought that comes when you have too much time on your hands. Do you recall the account of Mary sitting at the feet of Rabbi Jesus? You know the reason why she was there instead of helping with the work? She was weaker than Martha, that's why. It was Martha who greeted the guests and made them comfortable. It was she who ventured out when her brother Lazarus had died to meet Jesus and his party when they approached Bethany. Meanwhile, Mary weeps or sits dreamily at Jesus' feet to gain strength from him. "She has chosen the better part," Jesus said, rebuking Martha.

But why was it better? *Because Mary needed reassurance.* She was not a take-charge type that knows what to do and how to do it. Martha recognized Jesus as Messiah and believed he could save every situation. So she went about using her gift of hospitality, while Mary found what she needed. They were a matched pair. I don't think there is any basis for judging either of them harshly. You people who say "Someone around here has got to tend the store!" need to know you are valued. Without you, the Marys of the world would have no chance to sit at the Master's feet.

"What does that have to do with anything," you ask? Well maybe not much. But it may be something for us to ponder.

Item: Ajit came to see me last night at the Guest House. (Dave Walker, my missionary house mate, has more drop-bys than I do. But then, he is the color man around here—just going into rooms when there is a free period and asking if they want him to fill the time. The entire class stays—every time! He holds them spell-bound and they come for private advice.) Ajit is a vibrant, earnest early-twenties guy—so happy he is going to graduate in March and start as associate pastor at a church here in his home district. He comes from a solidly middle-class Hindu family, who wanted him to be a doctor. And he has enough smarts, no question. They have cast him out of the family since he gave his life to Christ. But he is happy to suffer for the one who suffered so for his rescue.

He plies me with many questions about how to be a good pastor. He already loves the people there so much. He wants to show them how to be co-ministers with him—to visit the sick and the poor in their afflictions and to reach out to Hindus and Muslims.

He says his goal is to write a book a year. Here's his plan. Gather a dozen people for weekly Bible study and encourage them to probe his teaching on a Bible book and then to put it to use. Then he can compile all that into a sort of collaborative Bible commentary. Naturally, I affirm his desire.

Then he starts asking about marriage. "What qualities does a pastor require in a wife?" Well that's right down my alley. I have a lot of wisdom in theory and lots of blessing in experience on that one.

Then he asks about a "man on campus" that has his sights on a girl who comes from a higher socio-economic station and he doesn't know if it is proper to seek her hand. Besides, she is several years younger than he and will be at New Theological College long after he graduates. How can he advise this man? After pointing out a few obvious cautions for him to use to advise this friend, he tells me "I am that man! I believe God has shown me this classmate is to be my wife!"

Hoo-boy...! Breathe deep here.

Ajit quickly comes to see that he needs to give her space to search her own heart. She must come to it on her own. (I've counseled people before in that kind of situation—usually in vain.) To my delight he says that he will not push but will wait for her to make an approach to him, since she knows how he feels about her already. "If she comes, then I know God is in it. If not, I will know God is not in it."

Bingo! I assure him that in this way he walks by faith. He will see ten years from now how the right path was already planned for him and he will have no regrets—no matter how it turns out.

Amazing. The guy with too much time on his hands actually made a difference in the real world—helping fix something so the real world is a little less broken.

Thanks, Bill. I know you were holding my rope and gently bringing me back to planet Earth.

Flunko, Flunkere, Flunki, Flunktus

Herewith I cause my Latin teacher of yore to spin in his grave as I create a bit of Latin doggerel that I think expresses a mood that overtakes one when an exam has been a disaster.

I do not recall if this came from the subterranean vaults of my deep (yea! now very, very deep) mind or if it was a byword of my mates at Roxbury Latin School (where I spent six very long years), whose motto is "*Mortui Vivos Docent.*" "The Dead Teach the Living." (Now there's a slogan for you!)

Lacrimosa. Another fitting word from the Romans. Yes—tears are threatening to overflow the dam that males have at the shores of their eyes. *Lacrimossissima*!

I gave a midterm yesterday and 90% of the class FLUNKED!

Incredible mishmash of clichéd concepts from mushy minds. If I had hair to spare I would sacrifice some to assuage my grief. Any professor knows that a failure of that magnitude is a failure of the teacher as well.

I must consult my never-failing books of *Helpful Advice*. Two volumes in this set—*What to Do* and *Don't Do It.*

Looking up *What to Do* I find an entry that says berate them roundly and apply the heat of public humiliation. *Don't Do It* warns against rash remedies designed to merely make the teacher feel better. Hmm....

What To Do suggests making them all come in the evening and re-sit the exam. *Don't Do It* mentions that doing the same thing again expecting different results is the first step toward insanity. Hmm....

These volumes of advice are not going anywhere. As a sagacious philosopher, I can grasp that the two volumes are designed to negate one another on every point.

Thrown upon my own devises, then....

I know! I will tear down my exam morgue and build a bigger one, then say to myself, *"Well done, you now have a superfluity of exam questions. Sit back, lay it on them again, and take your ease."*

Yipes! That means I'll have to grade another set of exams. Who am I punishing here?

Time for some deeper thinking....

Aha! I will cancel the second reading report (it tends to be meaningless copying of ideas from the textbook) and have them research answers to the mid-term and hand that in instead. That way they will correct their own mistakes, prepare themselves for the final exam, and make it easy for me to see improvements. I will tell them that at least two of the questions will re-appear on the final. That should motivate them with a carrot instead of a stick.

Meanwhile, I will give a lecture on how to write ideas that form a logical argument, thereby helping to drain the mush from their swampy minds and harden some dialectical bedrock as they climb the hills of higher learning.

I am smiling now, wiping the tears away, and looking for better things.

As Gilbert and Sullivan once put it in an operetta: *A Professor's Lot Is Not a Happy One.*

This marathon (a whole course in 12 days) is approaching Heartbreak Hill.

Take courage, my soul. There are many more tears ready to overflow the brim and wash your optimism away.

I'd give anything to stop that conjugation that keeps tormenting me.... *Flunko, flunkere, flunki, flunktus....*

Day by Day

MONDAY, NOVEMBER 6, 2006

Here at New Theological College in India, Sunday has a different flavor. Hindu and Muslim workmen are on the job, cities and towns bustle with commerce, while Christians flock to church. And while the Christian community is a small percentage of the population, the census puts India over the 1 billion mark as the world's most populous nation, resulting in there being a hefty number of those who claim to be followers of Christ despite the percentages.

As dawn emerges lazily through the haze hugging the mountains, I hear the clear tones of the bell at the Buddhist monastery just over the wall from the Guest House. More distant is the drone of traffic, the everlasting honking of horns, and clatter of machinery. Workmen are putting new Mediterranean red tiles on the office building. But for me, it is a day of worship.

I am privileged to be the preacher today. I arrive before 9 o'clock, meditating as people trickle in. Sunday School children occupy front seats facing the main congregation at a right angle. All of us are on plastic chairs such as we have on our patios for summer. By 9 o'clock the 250-seat room is full.

Part One

Student musicians take their places: two Yamaha keyboards, a drum set, bongos, plus guitar and bass. Professor Solomon Bison presides today. After a song we listen to his comments on Psalm 84. As he reads the text I hear the sublime setting of the text in Brahms' Requiem: *How lovely is thy dwelling place, O Lord of hosts. My soul longs, yea faints, for the courts of the Lord.... Even the sparrow has found her a house and the swallow a nest where she may lay her young, even thine altars, O God. Blessed are those who dwell in thy house, ever praising your name.*

I wonder what it was like for the Son of Korah who wrote this Old Testament song of praise, watching birds flying in and out of the Temple during the sacrifices in Jerusalem 3000 years ago.

Bison has a sweet, gentle air about him. He is Lecturer in Old Testament. An Indian man, with his spiky black hair he appears to have some oriental genes in his ancestry. His homily would be the main message back in the states—or even here in mainline denominations. But this community is charismatic—on the sane edge of Pentecostalism. So while there is seldom anything to make this Calvinistic Congregationalist uncomfortable, I know they are going to give us a three-course meal of spiritual food. Bison's is just the appetizer.

Now comes the serious praise music. 30 minutes of lively singing, switching seamlessly between Hindi and English. While I stand enjoying clapping the rhythms I suddenly realize I can sing the words now that English has hit the screen up front—but only for a season. The tempo quickens. The volume rises. Then "at the top of the ascent" it quiets to simultaneous mumbling prayers from the worshipers while the keyboard plays an ever more quiet background.

Part Two

This segment features announcements and a call for prayer requests. There are many. I hope the person who is going to be asked to pray is writing them down!

Two late-thirties women from Australia are introduced. They are specialists in disability remediation and are working at the prestigious Buddhist Library and Ashram a few blocks away. (That complex was dedicated a few years back by the Dalai Lama himself! Devotees now come from many places in the world to spend time in study and meditation—at luxury prices. The view of the Himalayan foothills here—a mere 8000 feet above sea level make a spectacular venue. And you could come if you have the bucks—it's not just for Buddhists.)

Now the kids come on stage, adjusting microphones so their squeaky voices can be heard. A few stumble over the cords as their protagonist yanks hers across the 10-foot platform. A plastic chair is set for the boy with a crown, holding a book in his lap: "*The Book of Life*." A girl approaches.

I have come to enter heaven.

You cannot go unless your name is in the Book of Life.

Will you check me, please?

What is your name?

Elise.

Abraham, Moses, David, Jonah....Elise! You may enter now.

Another girl approaches, same theme.

What is your name?

Iska

Mmmmm... I cannot find your name. Angel! Come take her to hell!

No! Oh! It is full of spiders and snakes and is too hot!

(She turns to see Elise going in the other direction.)

Elise, they are taking me to hell! I don't want. I was good – in fact you did more bad than I did. How did you get to go to heaven?

I confessed and took Jesus as Savior, so they wrote my name in the Book.

Announcer: *The moral is, accept Jesus as your personal Savior while there is yet time.*

Next comes the time for prayer from the brother who wrote down all those requests. He prays for 5 minutes fervently, mentioning each one and also for "Auntie and Uncle" (the founders of the college, George and Leela Chavinikamanil) and for the speaker of the morning, that hearts may be open to hear the Word of God.

I know it is OK to slip some US dollars into the velvet bag that the young lady stretches out along the rows. During the offering a male soloist sings a lively number accompanied by a keyboardist whose fills are unbelievable – he shifts patches skillfully to get saxophones, flute, sitars etc. into the mix of sounds. The principal, Dr. Samuel, had given a prayer of dedication to the new drum set and Yamaha—a gift of the North Shore Baptist Church in Massachusetts. "You have stored the old ones safely away, I trust," he said with a worried look. Nothing much is tossed out here.

Part Three

It's now an hour and a half into the service: my turn to open the Scriptures and preach the Gospel. I had chosen II Corinthians 5:1-9, focusing on verse 7: *we walk by faith and not by sight.* The translator was really good. We established a rhythm very quickly. Preaching this way gives one time to think a little more on one's feet while the Hindi echo is going forth. Words were flowing as I illustrated the text by the story of Phillemon Busolo, a Kenyan who attends West Church along with his wife and two boys.

Fast forward> > >

Just a few minutes ago a young man came by to share with me privately. He is the man who works with Dr. Timothy Tennent of Gordon-Conwell Theological Seminary in translating resources for ministry into Hindi (India's first official language)—a very gifted young man who also teaches here. I had him as a guest in class, where he shows how natural he is in communicating.

But he wanted to tell me his story. Born in central India, his mother died shortly after his birth. Other family members raised him as a charity project. His father was a teacher in the outback of India. They lived in a mud house about the size of a modest garage in the USA. Later his father took another young woman as "wife," so he now has two half-brothers.

When he was 15, orphaned and neglected and dreaming of Bollywood, he saw Jesus in a dream and gave his life to God. Raised Hindu, his family shunned him. So he had to rely on God to get an education, to come to this college, to meet and marry a young widow here (that, too is another touching story since widows with children have zero value in India) and to teach here.

But last February his father died—by witchcraft. Raised in rural India, he claims there is a lot of that going on. The perpetrators were his father's "wife" and another woman he kept in the household. Outcast and bereft, my friend was mourning deep within. Carrying on his work, no one knew the darkness creeping back into his soul. "I have no address. No house or land of my own. No family left." He was so low he hesitated to come even to church Sunday.

Then he heard me reading II Corinthians 5:1 "Now we know that if the earthly tent we live in is destroyed, we have a building from God, an eternal house in heaven not built by human hands. Meanwhile we groan, longing to be clothed with our heavenly dwelling...." God's spirit came over him. The sun broke through his depression and he was full of joy in his faith once again.

This, I tell myself, is why we are left on earth—to be instruments of blessing that God may use us, unworthy as we are, to let the love and grace of Christ bring hope and healing.

Day by day.

Yes, day by day God is good to his people.

As I sit on this sunny, cool day writing this at a computer in a specious four desk office in New Theological College's newest building, the girl at the desk, in her flowing sari, breezes in to ask, "Sir, would like to tehk some tea?" "Oh yes," I reply, "I missed the all-college tea time at 10:30 because I was online in the library." (You have to take Internet here when it is "awailable." So I had been locked in the library—literally— for 15 minutes while the staff went for tea.)

Soon a delicate cup of chai will be set on the edge of my desk. Maybe I could become a mahatma here in time if I work on it. I think I'm getting close. Life has its pleasant moments! Ah! Here it is now—wery vell. In less time than it takes to write a paragraph!

It has been quite a weekend.

An Infidel Defects to Secularism

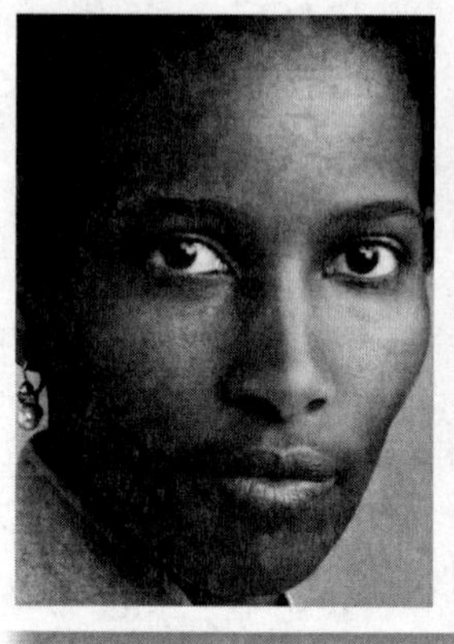

I want to center this lecture on humanism around the autobiography of Ayaan Hirsi Ali, "*Infidel*", published in 2007 by Free Press.

I find her story both fascinating and compelling. Fascinating because in a single lifetime she has recapitulated the historical development of humanity from ignorant tribalism to sophisticated enlightenment humanism. Compelling, because her story puts a vivid face on the implications of various world views.

Negatively, it shows repression of the human mind and spirit by unenlightened dogmatism.

Positively, it shows how the human spirit can flourish when blessed by the light of reason guiding the warmth of selfless love.

Ali grew up in Somalia in a tribal setting that Europeans began to outgrow over a thousand years ago. Her world view centered on the interaction of clans, fostering feelings of "us" versus "them." One tribe is superior to another, or inferior as the case may be, due to ancestry and their place in the pecking order of society. Its values centered on honor—everyone must act in ways that preserve the honor of the clan. Since tribalism is usually male-dominated, this meant that women and girls had no life they could call their own.

I know that there are tribal societies that are matriarchal rather than patriarchal. But Somali tribalism is embedded in an Islamic world view, where women are subservient to males. Her husband, her father, her brother, or a male relative within the clan, no matter how distant the relationship may be, must protect a wife or daughter.

One of the values of tribalism is a strong sense that one belongs. There is a strong organic connection.[2] As Somalis relate their ancestry back ten or more generations, they find a connection that makes them cousins and therefore qualified for care and protection. This is a significant benefit when disaster or displacement uproots someone. If one can find a clan connection, one is taken care of. It's a matter of honor.

On the other hand, such Islamic women must stay at home unless accompanied by a male. Daughters are expected to marry a person selected by the father, though some refuse. To go off on one's own, especially into non-Islamic relations, is to disgrace the family and the clan.

Since Islam is fixated on sexual sins, Somali clans blame females for lustful responses in males. Thus women must cover their skin and not even look men in the eye as this can inflame desire. This also explains the common African practice of excision of female genitals. Females are thought to be wanton and unable to control their sexuality. By cutting off either the clitoris or in some cases the entire genitalia, then sewing up what remains into a kind of tissue-based chastity belt, husbands can have proof their bride is a virgin.

2 In this context organic means that an individual has little value outside of his position in the group, as opposed to atomism that stresses the autonomy of each person as an individual.

Ayaan Hirsi Ali and her sister and cousins, as all Somali girls, suffered this mutilation and were supposed to be proud of it as an honored tribal custom. When the adolescent Ali asked a *ma'alim* (teacher of the Koran) why men didn't have to cover up since they can arouse passion in females, she was basically told to shut up and not challenge Islamic dogma.

This is standard for tribal cultures. And religions often take a long time to emerge from the cocoon of dogmatism, wriggling out into the light of reason. Judaism and Christianity began to become self-analytical millennia ago and its mainstream branches are comfortable with self-criticism. This is due to the influence of Greek philosophy that has shaped European thought since the Renaissance. But this is not yet true for Islam. Islam is still in a tribal stage of development in that it accepts its world view and Koranic dogma without question. In fact, it is usually antagonistic to any challenge to the truth of its claims.

In tribal cultures, questioners are simply told: *It's the ancient way of our ancestors.* Trans-tribal dogmatic religions likewise appeal to authority. *"God punishes those who doubt and who keep asking skeptical questions."*

Now while this still persists at some level in Christianity and Judaism, scholars in these traditions have largely come to examine the foundations of their respective world views in terms of rational criteria. Is the Bible the Word of God? Did the events foundational to faith—such the Exodus of the Hebrews under Moses, or the life, teaching, and resurrection of Jesus—actually take place? What is fact and what is fiction? What is coherent and what is incoherent? These are questions getting major attention in religions that have evolved beyond tribalism and dogmatism. But Islamic tribalism has not yet attained to this level of maturity.

When Ali found herself in Europe in the 1990s, she found herself in a world beyond her comprehension. She was shocked by it; she was enthralled by it.

Fleeing as a refugee from the bloodshed going on in Somalia, she found people in Holland, where she applied for asylum, were helpful to her. She was not of their clan. She was not of their religion. There was no tribal precedent for their treating her other than as dirt—such as she had encountered in Kenya and Saudi Arabia where her family had briefly located. Her tribal mindset had no explanation for this in its world view.

Ali later came to understand that this came from the influence of enlightenment ideas and the example and teaching of Jesus Christ. All people were created by God and should love one another—even enemies. She found that police were not enemies out to hurt you if you did not give bribes. She was given housing, food, and even cash pocket money while she awaited her interviews. Government workers were solicitous of her feelings and showed genuine concern for her as an individual. When she dared to wear western clothes, showing her neck, arms and ankles, no one took notice. Men did not ogle her and pounce upon her with uncontrollable lust as she expected due to her religious training and from the way unprotected girls were treated in Somalian culture.

Ali did not know it at the time, but she was enjoying the benefits of humanism.

Humanism in the West came from Christian scholars such as Erasmus. Its roots are two-fold: the probing method of classical Greek philosophy and the equality of all humans derived from Jesus Christ. Having embraced the former, can Ayaan Hirsi Ali find her way to the latter—to a Creator who, rather than demanding we sacrifice for him, sacrificed himself for us? If so, she will experience the love of God that passes all human understanding.

Damned If You Do or Damned If You Don't?

This is intended as more than a play on words, much less as a joke.

I intend it to be a catchy way of remembering a significant difference among religions as to the way of salvation. I do not intend this as an attack on any religious world view but as a clarification of a key point in every religious and non-religious world view. Every world view is giving an answer to the quest for salvation that has been with the human race from as far back as one can trace our origins.

Archeologists speculate concerning pre-historic human beliefs about life and the afterlife on the basis of artifacts such as burial mounds and human remains unearthed from many sites around the globe.

We focus here on religions that still survive in our times.

Eastern religions like Buddhism and Hinduism teach that our destiny is determined by our deeds, whether good or bad. The law of reward and retribution causes a soul to either move upward toward liberation from the cycle of rebirths or downward. At the end, the soul escapes re-incarnation and dissolves into the timeless One (Brahman) where there is no further suffering since there is no further personal consciousness. The curse of multiple births into this world is the hell we must endure until our debt of karma is paid in full. One can say, then, that one is saved and damned by one's deeds. There is no slack given, no mercy, no grace from on high. Brahman is not aware of our struggles to achieve salvation—nirvana.

Judaism is the oldest of monotheistic world views, dating from Abraham approximately 4,000 years ago. It has developed over the centuries into a small but vital religion. Religious Judaism teaches that the righteous will find the rewards of heaven if one's life merits the commendation of God. One is saved based on one's works, whether good or evil. One is damned if one persists in doing evil and saved if one succeeds in being righteous in the eyes of God.

As Maimonides put it, *I believe with perfect faith that the Creator, Blessed be His Name, rewards those who keep His commandments and punishes those that transgress them.*

Islam is the latest of the great monotheistic religions, purporting to be the culmination of faith that stems from Abraham and on through Jesus and the Apostles of Christianity. Like Judaism, Islam teaches that one is saved by one's deeds. If one's good deeds outweigh those done out of ignorance, one may be granted entrance into Paradise where pleasures of food, wine, and companionship are fulfilled.

For Islam, people are not so much willfully sinful as ignorant, often making many mistakes. But faithful obedience to the pillars of the faith can assure one a place in the world to come—with one exception. Allah, being sovereign, is not obligated to reward anyone with salvation. Even the most righteous person could be sent to hell should Allah will it. However, if one avoids *shirk*[3] and follows devoutly the way of Islam, one will avoid damnation and can hope for salvation and entrance into Paradise.

Christianity is the odd religion on this topic, teaching that one's deeds can never bring one to salvation, only to perdition. Since all our self-styled righteous works are offensive to God, every act only seals one's doom. How can this be?

Because the works we do in an attempt to justify us before God are motivated by prideful self-seeking. Only deeds done with a pure heart cleansed of all taint of sin are acceptable to God. And there are none such. We stand in a position of rebellion against God and our good works cannot overcome the condition of our hearts. Good and evil works alike damn us. Good works can never save us. This idea is counter-intuitive and often incomprehensible to many. How then can one be rescued?

As a person who sins in thought, word, and deed one is saved by throwing oneself upon the mercy of God. My relationship with God must be healed first. Otherwise it is futile to try to clean myself up. This requires repentance and total trust in the provision of God to transform the heart through the work of Jesus Christ, who died for our sins and rose to bring new life to all who believe.

---

3 According to Wikipedia, *shirk* is the sin of idolatry, i.e. the deification or worship of anyone or anything other than the singular God, or more literally the establishment of "partners" placed beside God. Within Islam, *shirk* is an unforgivable crime.

Good works then are not a *means of salvation* but a *grateful response to salvation* that is freely given as a *gift*, not because of works of righteousness that we have done but in virtue of his mercy. (See the New Testament, Titus 3:5)

Works can only damn us, not save us. Grace alone can save us, with works following as a result of the salvation that is provided as a gift from God through faith. Faith without works is dead, says the Apostle James. But works cannot raise the dead. We are dead in our sins so far as salvation goes. God kindly provides forgiveness and the life of eternal salvation, even helping us to repent of our rebellious attitude toward Him.

We start out already condemned and we continue to be damned no matter if we do or we don't. Salvation is a gift not a reward. I am damned if I do or if I don't as far as my salvation is concerned. This does not mean that it does not matter what I do in this life, since my actions have social effects that are good and bad in that context.

But when it comes to preparing oneself to meet God, a different set of standards applies.

Some may say this is a cheap free ride. But Christianity teaches the opposite. True faith means turning over one's entire life 24/7 to God, seeking always to serve God's program and not one's own plan for life.

It's like being on active duty. You serve the will of the Commander 100% of the time.

On this central point Christianity is distinct from other religious world views.

East and West

How can we explain the significant difference between what are often called Eastern religions and Western monotheistic religions?

One answer may be that eastern religions are primarily ethical while monotheisms are primarily metaphysical (explaining the nature of what is real—what kind of a universe do we live in).

This bears explanation.

While it is obvious that all religions (and even secular humanism) combine both ethics and metaphysics, the monotheistic religions draw their ethical requirements from the metaphysical structure of reality—the metaphysical has priority. The eastern religions paint a metaphysical background to support their moral claims—the ethical has priority.

The sages of the east, from the origins of Hinduism to Buddhism to Confucius and others, focused on how one should behave in society as the first concern. Duties to one's family, friends and society at large are paramount. Be a good citizen, a good friend, a good father or mother, son or daughter.

Eastern mythology paints a backdrop of what the universe is in order to support these ethical claims. From the Vedas to Taoism's Tao Te Ching and even Confucius' references to Heaven's Mandate there is little concern as to whether the sagas and descriptions of the Ultimate Reality are factual. It is one's duty that is foremost. The nature of the universe is secondary.

In the monotheistic religions and in the secular world view the prime concern is to discern the nature of the universe at large. As Thomas Cahill has argued in ***The Gifts of the Jews***, Abraham was the first to successfully promote a linear view of history rather than a cyclical view as is found in eastern philosophy.

For eastern religions the universe proceeds in endless cycles. The basic metaphysical conditions that support the human quest for meaning are almost irrelevant. Humans are reborn in countless cycles until they achieve ethical perfection, whereupon they cease to exist as individuals, merging with The One in an existence that is neither spatial nor temporal.

In the western view history is linear, having a beginning, a middle, and an end.

The western view says that the universe was created at a precise time in the past—perhaps some 13 billion years go. Our study of the dynamics of the universe enables us to predict an end of history as we know it when the sun explodes. In the end the universe winds down some billions of years in the future. Meanwhile, we live somewhere in the middle.

Because of this linear view of reality, western thought derives its ethics in keeping with this world view. Life is not a cycle of suffering that one hopes to be relieved of. Life is an opportunity to engage in the drama of cosmic history. One strives to live an ethical life in order to enjoy the beauty and wisdom of God long after life on this planet is over. Rather than achieving a release from individual conscious life, one seeks an enhancement of life, in which the individual reaches a higher awareness of the universe and the One who has created it. A single lifetime on this planet is all we need to secure our place in the unfolding story of creation.

Secular humanism arose in this western context. Humans, say humanists, have one lifetime in which to arrive at ethical fulfillment. Secularism of course denies that life goes on after death. But the arrow of time proceeds in one direction, whether one believes in immortality of the individual or not. There is no evidence that humans cycle through countless lives on this planet as some eastern religions insist. We get only one chance. For the secularist we must get whatever we can before we die and suffer the extinction of the self. For the theist we must live in such a way as to prepare ourselves for life on a higher plane - a new heaven and a new earth. But that future world will consist of space and time and personal experiences.

This explains why monotheists believe in the resurrection of each person to face a verdict as to their place in the higher level of life that is coming. One's ethical achievements show what that destiny is to be. But the significant difference is that an individual persists in the future timeline fully cognizant of his or her prior experience. By contrast, in eastern cyclical world views the individual's goal is to cease existing as an individual altogether. To be sure, there are exceptions to these details among some permutations of eastern religions. But this is true as a generalization.

The ethical systems of monotheism arise from the wider concept of its linear metaphysical world view. The metaphysical views of eastern thought are created to support its ethical requirements. In the West reality determines ethics. In the East ethics determines reality.

Is reality on a linear track with a one-directional trajectory?

Or is reality on a circular track that goes around and around forever?

To grasp this difference provides insight into these diverse world views. If we wish to analyze the comparative credibility of each system one must scrutinize the underlying (and to most people invisible) assumptions of epistemology—how does one sort out what counts for knowledge? That is a longer story for another article.

Jonathan Edwards: Do We Have Freewill?

Jonathan Edwards took a walk in the woods, looking for spiders, when he tripped over a question.[4] It's a question many of us have encountered.

If God has ordained everything from before the foundation of the world, how can my choices make any difference? If a name is either written in the *Book of Life* or not written there long before that name was given to a newborn boy or girl, how can he or she be held accountable for not making it to salvation?

4 Jonathan Edwards, 1703-1758, is considered by scholars to be early America's most brilliant mind. He wrote voluminously, starting with an essay on the habits of flying spiders when he was 11 years of age. Pastor of the congregational church in Northampton, Massachusetts, his preaching sparked the first Great Awakening in the American colonies in 1735.

This conundrum has been around a long time—how to reconcile the free will of man and the sovereign will of God.

Those of us who stand in the Reformed tradition know some powerful minds that have wrestled with this—Augustine and Jonathan Edwards among them.

In what follows I do not pretend to untie this Gordian knot but merely to suggest that a lot has changed in our understanding of the world since these intellectual giants engaged the subject. I believe this new understanding requires a paradigm shift that may send us in a new direction as we seek to answer this question, often posed by new believers as well as seasoned saints.

To do this we must back up and search for some tools that can help us talk about this. In my dissertation on freedom of the will I found that Edwards was classified as a *soft determinist.* Let me explain what that means before I argue that his view, though brilliant for his time, needs revision.

Return with me now to the woods near Northampton, Massachusetts.

Story I: The dilemma

Edwards does not see any spiders this morning. But he does see a young man approaching along the footpath.

"Good morning, Mr. Edwards! I hope you do not mind my interrupting you, but I have been watching you walking about here in our hills for some hours now and was afraid you might be distraught over something that burdens you regarding the church situation."

"Oh, good morning, Christopher. No, not at all. Ever since my jottings about the habits of the spider, done when I was but a boy of 11, I come often to meditate and to praise the Creator of these wonders here in the woods—quite forgetting the passage of time! I am quite well, actually, caught up as I am just now in the glories of our God!"

" I am glad of it! But if you don't mind, Sir, I have been waiting to pose a question for you."

"Is that so? Pray speak on and I will answer as best I can."

"Thank you, Parson. Here is my dilemma. If God is the cause of all things and truly knows the future actions of all men, how can he hold me accountable for my choices? Has he given us freewill or no?"

"An excellent question, my lad. I will attempt to give you insight as God helps me."

At this juncture Edwards goes on to make several salient points.

Foundational to his reply are these ideas.

First, God is sovereign over all of creation and has pre-ordained all that comes to pass. Second, God knows everything that has occurred and that ever will occur in the universe he has created. This means that a person who chooses to do X could never have done Y in its stead. This view is known as determinism—an effect is determined by its causes.

Edwards continues on to derive from these first principles the only concept of freewill that accomplishes the two things needed in a Reformed theology of human life. The first is that everything is pre-ordained, even the slightest minutia of each human life. The second is that God justly holds us accountable for actions that have moral elements.

By the first, Edwards comes under the category of determinism as we have said. Whatever happens is completely determined by its causes. Given the fact, for example, that Cain was angry with Abel and that an opportunity presented itself in the field, his killing his brother was the only act that could have come to pass. That is determinism. Whatever happens is the only thing that could happen because the causes make it happen.

But Edwards is a *soft* determinist. That means he must provide a basis for moral accountability. Even though Cain's act was determined, Cain is still morally responsible for it and can justly be punished for it.

At this point, Chris cannot keep silent. "But he couldn't help it! How can God punish him if he couldn't have dropped the rock or just walked away or done some alternative act? He had to do it, you say, due to the causes at work. God foreknew it. God foreordained it!"

Edwards explains that as long as Cain wanted to do what he did, he is accountable and can be punished. It was his act, after all. If Satan had come along and moved Cain's hand against Cain's wishes so that he unwillingly killed Abel, then it would not be Cain's fault because it would not be Cain's act. But since the act flowed out of Cain's heart—it was something he *wanted* to do—he is accountable.

We sin because we want to. It flows out of our own nature. Sure, our nature is perverted. But our wills express what is in our hearts. Our actions are *our* actions.

"But that doesn't seem to agree with my experience," objects young Christopher. "Many times I sense that I can as easily put this pebble into my pocket as throw it down to the ground. I can do either one. It's up to me, isn't it?" says he, tossing it in the air.

"Yes," replies Edwards, "it seems so. But many things are not as they seem to the casual observer. For example, the sun seems to set, but since Copernicus we know that it does not. So also it seems that we can do X as easily as Y. But that does not make sense in moral situations.

"For example, if Cain could have stayed his hand, despite the rage in his heart, how do we explain that he killed Abel? If his inclinations could have gone either way, then it seems there is no reason why Cain killed him rather than not—a capricious act. But how can God, or anyone, blame someone for a capricious act that has no definable cause? We cannot say 'because Cain chose to do it.' We need to know *why* Cain chose to do it instead of doing some other act. Only then could we hold him accountable. If either X or Y could come about with the causes being exactly the same, then we have no basis for blaming Cain for what he did. We blame Cain because the causes foaming in his sinful heart *necessitated* the brutal murdering of his brother."

"I suppose you are right, Sir, but it seems strange nonetheless, to my way of thinking."

"That may be," replies Edwards, "but God knew Cain would murder Abel long before creation began. And Cain is justly accountable for what he did, even though it was all determined ahead of time according to the way the Grand Scheme of the Universe was designed to play out."

Analysis

Let's stop here and evaluate Edwards' response to Chris.

Do you think Edwards gave a satisfactory answer? Unsatisfactory?

I will argue for *unsatisfactory* on the following grounds.

In doing so I do not fault Edwards for his answer. I think he did the best he could with what he had to work with. And I don't mean his intellectual firepower. Edwards is arguably still the most brilliant philosophical mind America has produced. I am referring rather to the reigning paradigm of the Newtonian era in which Edwards lived. Edwards, as all intellectuals in the European tradition, was imbued with the new conception of the world so brilliantly conceived by Isaac Newton a generation earlier.

Newton conceived nature as working according to fixed scientific laws—gravitation, thermodynamics, entropy, etc. It's pretty much what Donald McKay said in his Inter-Varsity Press booklet, *Clockwork Image*. God made the clock, set the clock, and watches the clock. It's a paradigm of celestial mechanics.

But since Einstein and Heisenberg, a new paradigm has informed our understanding of nature and hence of ourselves as created beings within nature. Being a pastor and philosopher (as Edwards also was) I am no expert in science and will not pretend to make more than suggestions to be taken forward by others with more knowledge than I have.

Story II: A Way Out of the Dilemma

I was walking in my forest in Vermont not long ago and saw a man coming along the logging road. In our conversation, after I told him I was a philosophy professor, he asked if I had any knowledge of Jonathan Edwards.

"Actually I do, having written a dissertation that included some of his ideas."

"Great!" he replied. "You see, one of my great-great-great-grandfathers knew Edwards when he was minister in Northampton. Since then some of us have wandered north, now living here in Vermont."

"You're kidding! One of your ancestors knew Edwards?" I exclaim. "That's fantastic!"

"Yes, it is. We are very proud of our connection. And we have a story written by one Christopher about his questions concerning freewill that Edwards answered one day when they met out in the woods. But none of us have been any more satisfied with it than Christopher was in 1738."

He went on to recount the episode above. He wondered if anything had come to light in the last several centuries that might provide a more satisfactory answer to the freewill conundrum.

"Actually there is," I replied. "If you have a some time, come over to the cabin where we can sit on the glider with some iced tea and I'll tell you what I think Edwards might say now."

So we sat down to swing, iced tea in hand, while enjoying the dappled sunlit foliage.

"Edwards did the best one could, given the thought forms of the 18th Century," I began.

"You see, in the days of Newtonian physics, brilliant at the time, the universe was thought of in mostly mechanical terms—potential and kinetic energy, the laws of the conservation of energy, and all that sort of thing. Edwards tried to explain human action using that paradigm. But now we have had a paradigm shift, one that I find a bit baffling, to be honest with you. But since most physicists accept it, I think we can use it. And it provides new ways of thinking about freewill."

"What in particular?" asked Chris.

"Let me give you an example," I replied.

"Einstein says that time is relative to the observer. If one could move fast enough, time would stand still. I have no clue what that would be like. But maybe it can explain how God, if he is faster than the speed of light, can see what we do as we do it, even though we, in the slow tunnel of time, are not even there yet to do it!"

"Oh. Wow!" said Chris XII, "that's a cool way to think about it!"

"Yes. And Heisenberg said that the principle of indeterminacy allows some events that would seem strange to Newton. For instance, you cannot measure both the velocity and the location of a particle at the same time. Now Newton never had any idea of these particles—these gluons and bosons and morons—whatever they are. Anti-matter. String theory. The world God has created has a lot of things that don't fit a mechanical model at all."

"OK, I agree so far. But how does this relate to Cain killing Abel and all that?"

"Well," said I, "the human self may not be just another piece of the clockwork."

"A human self, like God, does not exhaust itself when doing an act. If I toss a pebble, all the energy I put into my throw will be used up in how far the pebble goes. But that is not the case when I am deciding whether to toss the pebble or not."

"A person may be able to select among the causal influences present in a given situation and bring about any one of several outcomes. For persons, there may be a degree of indeterminacy. Maybe Cain could have walked away. He had a choice. He chose to shape the influences within him in a certain way, and so he killed his brother. He may have been able to shape those same influences in another way had he chosen to do so. That does not mean his act is capricious or unexplainable as determinists fear. A self is a super-causal agent, unlike a stick of dynamite where everything is predictable in Newtonian terms."

"Our moral accountability is grounded in this special capacity that we have as persons made in the image of God. God knows what we will choose because he is in the future watching us. But God's knowing does not take away our free will."

"Would you also apply this idea to God?" asked Chris. "He is a person, too...."

"Good question!"

"Perhaps we can assume God also had real options; he did not have to create this world because of some inner necessity. Do you agree?"

"Seems logical," replied Chris.

"God has super-capacities. When God touched off the Big Bang, God did not exhaust all his potential into kinetic energy as happens when dynamite explodes. So we, made in his image, have the same super-capacity on a smaller scale. When we choose to do something, we do not have to expend all our potential any more than God does. This is called super-abundant causal agency."

"Does this mean that God is morally accountable for choosing to touch off the Big Bang and everything that would follow from it?" asked Chris.

"I don't know about that—although it does seem reasonable, remembering that God would only be accountable to Himself," I replied. "But it certainly applies to us humans."

"Thus we are held accountable for what we choose to do because we are not necessitated by causes that are beyond our shaping. Within the parameters of our finiteness we have real open-ended choices. God sees us doing those actions that are future to us because he is outside of time and is already there to see what we will have chosen. Just as he saw what Cain would freely choose to do."

" I think I am beginning to grasp your point," said Chris.

"Maybe this is an aspect where God's thoughts are higher than our thoughts," I continued, "as Edwards surely admitted. We know that Edwards revered the mysteries of God—mysteries not because they are absurd but because they are infinite. And if he had lived today, might he have answered differently than he did then? I am suggesting that there are categories beyond soft determinism and indeterminism that open to us new ways of thinking even within our Reformed tradition. Maybe the new paradigm can help us in other debates between Calvinists and Arminians."

"Well, that is something to ponder," he said, sucking on the last ice cube in his tumbler of tea. "I consider myself in the Reformed wing of Christian theology, as were my forebears. It's nice to have a new window to look through. Maybe it illustrates what another of our fathers-in-the-faith, John Winthrop, said: "There is yet more light to break forth from God's Word."

"Keep me in your prayers, Chris," I asked, shaking his hand. "I plan to say something along this line to our Congregational brethren (and sisteren) at an upcoming conference. Maybe I can start a dialog that will help us as we try to answer these persistent questions."